south pole epic

Daniel Burton

Assisted by Tip Boxell

Dedicated to Lynda Boone, my mother.

One year before my expedition, she went out to feed her chickens and never came back. I have spent the last seven years of my life in the pursuit of helping others to live a healthy lifestyle so that they will not have to die before their time.

Acknowledgments

Many people made this expedition and this book possible. I may have been alone in Antarctica, but this was really a team effort. So I want to thank:

Media and my family—my wife Media and my family have had to put up with my crazy ideas. For some reason they let me pursue this dream. It was great to be able to call them during the expedition and receive their love and support.

Jake, Greg, John, Joel, Steve, Ron, and Myron—they took care of my store while I was gone for over two months.

Myron—my son Myron has spent more time working at the store than anyone else. There were many times that he saved me by helping me get caught up with all the repair work. A great son, a great bike shop "employee," and my best biking buddy.

Antarctic Logistics and Expeditions—I could not have done it without the help of ALE. I spent countless hours talking with them on the phone planning for the expedition. Their base camp on Union Glacier was great, and of course their support during the expedition was essential.

Eric Larsen—who paved the way for me to do my expedition. He proved that a bike could be used in Antarctica and was the inspiration for my expedition.

Kendall and Lisa Bohman, Media Burton, and Tina Burton—for their editorial work on this book.

Tip Boxell—for taking my blog, journal, and interviews and turning them into a book. Those that know my writing style and those that know Tip's writing style may understand who wrote what. To everyone else the book was "written by Daniel Burton with the assistance of Tip Boxell."

Sponsors and Donors

Energy Solutions, Borealis Fat Bikes, Shimano, DHL, SatPhone Store, ReadyStore, Skinz Protective Gear, Pearl iZumi, Expedo, Bear River Outfitters, Hydro Flask, Tifosi, Canada Goose.

Brian MacLeod	Margaret Boone	Lynn LeBaron	Ross Poulton	David Lifferth
Richard Epperson	Zoe Jacobson	Doug Davies	Matthew Haight	Cheryl L. Karr
Jeff Perlman	Steve Hart	V. Trent Jackson	Thanyarat Doksone	Jake Weber
Shon Vella	Douglas B. McKay	Njall	David Crookston	Gregory Smith
Bob Bedore	Kim Thomson	Mary S. Mason	Daniel Peterson	David Murphy
Larry Johnson	Teresa Young	Kathleen Fueston	Kimberly Moody	Woody McCubbins
Christopher	Jeremy Berglund	Dan Christensen	Pam Robello	Kerry Collins Hicken
Dennis Stafford	Scott Henderson	Royce Van Tassell	Scott	Danae Burton
Christie Pratt	Lance Raven	Sam	Garrett Winn	Michael Downey
Jason Haskell	Ben Schmalz	Levi Cress	Chip Page	Junaid Ahmed
Eric Reese	Bret Rosenberg	Camille Slaughter	Mark Pendelton	Brian Blacka
Michael Lewis	David Mouritsen	Angela Mouritsen	Melissa Nicholson	Joel Quinn
Kelton Keller	Patrick Schooler	Lori Christensen	Brianna Curran	Nate Burt
Jim Erwin	Cindy Kingsley	Mason Swier	John Stohlton	Cheryl Emal
Cindy Kingsley	Mike Gressmen	Carl Wall	Tony Curtis	Mat
Mike Shepherd	Daniel Smith	Jared Allen	JD Tueller	Mike Downey
Dave Norman	James Haws	Chip Maldonado	Troy Reynolds	TJ Stone
Jennifer Doolittle	Juan Carlos Luciani	Rob McDonald	Chan Head	Blair Sears
Jason Kirkpatrick	Kelly & Brant Judy	Tiana Secor	Mark Chesley	Nichole Craig
Mike	Kami Orr	Heather Cannon	Shawn Beddes	Jeromy Nielson
Andrew Smith	Lisa Barkdull	Lamoni Parry	Darren Jorgensen	Aaron Crosby
Valerie Best	Stan & Lily Roberts	Nanette Keck	Ben Kuhlman	John Wallace
Jarom Smith	Hoa Quinn	Trevor Clifton		

CONTENTS

At the South Pole

Drop off at Hercules Inlet

The sign read, "The world's southernmost resort," but it didn't look anything like a resort. Daniel Burton, from Eagle Mountain, Utah, stopped pedaling his fat tired bicycle through the snow. He didn't have to apply brakes, because the snow and the two supply sleds dragging behind him brought the bike instantly to a stop, which was fortunate because Daniel had long ago taken the brakes off his "snow bike." This was the non-governmental organization (NGO) camp site for expeditions arriving at the South Pole. The day before it had been a bustling hub of activity.

Now all that remained were the indentations in the ice left behind by other expeditions' tents and a large hole in the ice where a dining tent had been. Had Daniel arrived the day before, the big dining tent would have greeted him with a cozy place to eat. He would have loved to have been able to sit down and eat some soft warm cookies and drink some hot

1

chocolate and then eat a nice warm meal. Instead, he disconnected his sleds and continued south to the South Pole marker, a stick in the ice with an emblem on top. Daniel pulled out his inReach (a satellite tracking device) and sent a quick message just to document that he had arrived. Just a little north of the marker (duh, everything is north of the marker) was a sign that read:

Geographic South Pole

Roald Amundsen   **Robert F. Scott**

December 14, 1911   January 17, 1912

"So we arrived and were able to plant our flag at the geographic South Pole."   "The Pole. Yes, but under very different circumstances from those expected."

Elevation 9,301 feet

A little further north was another pole in the ground. This one was a bit fancier with red and white stripes, like a barber's pole, and a mirrored ball on top. Surrounding the pole were flags from the Antarctic Treaty signatory nations. This was the ceremonial South Pole, but there was no ceremony here today. Daniel had been alone for 51 days, but if ever he had felt lonely it would have been then. Behind the ceremonial South Pole was the Amundsen-Scott South Pole Station. Since all time zones converge at the South Pole, a visitor can pick any time zone to keep track of time. To Daniel it was noon, but the South Pole Station operates on New Zealand time, so for the permanent staff it was four in the morning and everyone was still in bed. He rode over to the ceremonial South Pole for a quick look, and continued back to his sleds.

He called his wife, Media, back home in Utah and, through the exhaustion and the numbing cold, suddenly lost all control of his emotions. He told her he was all right and at the South Pole. Media, by the way, is pronounced "mah-DEE-ya." When Daniel explains the pronunciation of his wife's name, he always reminds the listener that "Medea was not a nice person," whereas his wife, Media, is a wonderful

Ceremonial South Pole

person. Indeed, it should also be pointed out that in classic Greek mythology, Medea was the daughter of King Aeëtes who fell in love with the explorer adventurer, Jason, and helped him in his quest for the Golden Fleece just as Media helped her explorer adventurer in his quest now fulfilled.

Later, he blogged out a simple thought to his nation of followers.

Thanks for following me as I biked to the South Pole. Remember to get out and be active.

It was bitter cold, just as every other day in Antarctica, and yet he was drenched in sweat from a straight 24 hours of biking, all day and all through the previous "night." Yes, soaked, because pedaling over hard ice granules or pushing through soft powder snow worked up a sweat even in these cold temperatures. Although the sun is always up in late January at the height of the Antarctic summer, it was about -10° Fahrenheit at the coast, where he'd started 51 days ago, and about -35° Fahrenheit here, at the South Pole.

Daniel Burton had started his expedition as a slender man, built like a bird – all long muscles and bones, with the thinnest layer of insulating body fat. Now, he looked frighteningly skinny without an ounce of fat.

He wore a relatively light weight, bright red jacket. It provided high visibility which would make it easy to be seen in the event of a search and rescue. The jacket and his pants had vents that could be zipped open to provide ventilation to keep from getting too sweaty.

He wasn't dressed as he would dress for cycling back home in Utah. In summer back there, he wore spandex shorts and a polyester mesh knit jersey. On his head would be a light weight and well vented helmet. On his feet: light weight, cleated, mountain biking shoes. In his home biking clothes, he'd be dead in an hour out here on the ice. As it was, his external poplin shell was as cold as the still air, while his thin base layer clothes were soaked with perspiration from his intense burst of effort here at the end of the expedition.

So now he could not stop and enjoy his accomplishment. To stay alive he had to get his tent set up and get inside. When he finally got under shelter, he wanted to go and find the cache of items that had been left for him at the South Pole, but going outside his tent, even just long enough to grab the GPS off of his bike, would have been too much time in the bitter cold. The next day, probably in the same cold, he would be able to go out and find his stuff and the cold wouldn't bother him; being dry made all the difference.

One day before, on January 20, 2014, Daniel had reached the plateau around the crest of the 9,000 foot thick ice sheet over the Antarctic continent by pedaling or pushing a highly specialized, fat tired, snow bike with two nylon-plastic blue sleds behind him, mounded with his gear and supplies. Once he started cycling for the day, he could not stop to rest longer than the time it took to put a foot down and catch his breath, grab a drink and a handful of energy food, or to stop pushing and look around from the crest of a sastrugi. If he actually stopped, if he dared to sit down, he would freeze solid very quickly.

Whenever he stopped for the "night" (the sun never sets during the Antarctic summer, instead it just makes a big circle around the sky), he would pitch his tent, crawl inside, strip off his wet cycling clothes, and don his heavily quilted, fur lined down parka. Next he would carefully arrange his Antarctic bicycling clothes beside himself to allow the solar radiation to dry his clothes.

Sitting in the tent, he would pull off his highly specialized snow boots rated for -79° Fahrenheit. Normally he would ride a bike with shoes specially designed to lock into the pedals allowing every bit of energy produced to be transferred into making the bike go forward. In Antarctica, however, warmth was more important than efficiency so he was using large platform pedals that would accommodate the bulky (but warm) boots. When inside, the boots were placed at the head of his warm tent with the inner liners pulled out to allow them to dry. When outside, he looked bulky and stiff in his Antarctic clothing, like an Antarctic penguin, in fact.

Imagine a penguin riding a bicycle, but not just any bicycle. Daniel's black Borealis "Fat Bike," had been provided to his South Pole Epic expedition as the ultimate snow bike. With 26 inch wheels and 100 mm (4 inch) wide rims and 4.8 inch wide tires, the Borealis Fat Bike was a descendent of the original snow bike concept developed by the great cyclist explorer, Douglas Stoup, who had invented an "ice bike" with 20 inch wheels and 8 inch wide fat tires. The Borealis snow bike had larger diameter tires making it easier to roll over the rough Antarctic terrain. Doug's early ice bike was one of the first used in an attempt to bike in Antarctica with plans to someday bike to the South Pole. The bike Daniel used had many improvements that were developed in the years since Doug's ice bike.

Now, on January 21, 2014, it was over and Daniel had to survive the last little confusing time at the end of the ride.

The situation made Daniel think about alienation. He couldn't know that his thoughts and feelings at South Pole Station were the same as those of all combat veterans or missionaries or survivors or graduating students coming from their new world back to their old world. Daniel thought of something that had happened to one of his children. As every

good explorer/adventurer/expeditionary must do, Daniel had documented his achievement in Antarctica with all the electronic tools of today and also the ancient tool of the handwritten journal. He was taught to do this by his discipline as an explorer of self on his expedition, but also by his culture and his religion. As he tried to rejoin the society of mankind, he remembered what he wrote a decade before. It was appropriate in this existential moment.

From the Journal of Daniel Burton – 31 March 2002:

> At church today one of the speakers used the word alienate. Danae [Daniel's daughter] asked me what it meant. Then Myron [his son] asked what 99 meant. I told him it was a 9 and a 9. So he asked what 9 and 9 was. I told him ninety-nine. We went back and forth a couple of times. Not getting anywhere, Myron asked what eighty-eight was. So we went back and forth on that for a while. Then he said, 'No, what did you tell Danae that eighty-eight was?' It took me a second; then I realized that instead of alienate he had heard eight-eight.

An Alien at the South Pole. There were people there. They were in the station just across the base from the NGO camp that had been "struck" as the circus people say. Before any expedition could go to the station, it had to set up a time and appointment with ALE (Antarctic Logistics and Expeditions). You are not allowed to approach the station without an appointment. This could be very bad if you came in off the ice after a couple of months out there alone and you are now out of food and water, but the organized Daniel had his appointment and he presented himself, hairy and filthy in his bright red bulky clothes, to the person designated as the station tour guide for the day. During the tour the rest of the residents of the station mostly stayed concerned with their own work.

From the Journal:

> One day later Vesa arrives at the pole. We get a tour of the South Pole Station, and then a couple hours later the ALE plane shows up and takes us back to Union Glacier.

Who is Vesa? At the beginning of the Antarctic expedition season of Antarctic Summer, 2013-2014, Jaakko Heikka, superb Finnish wilderness guide and very professional student of lightweight backpacking, Arctic expeditions, and outdoor photography reported on his personal blog:

The season of science, adventure and publicity stunts is about to start once again at the Antarctica. Quality armchair adventuring is great for the quiet shoulder season and I enjoy it just as much as everyone else. Here are some chosen adventures happening on the great white continent of superlatives right now or about to start very soon.

Now, in late January, 2014, the expedition was over and Jaakko went on:

This one isn't a world-class ground breaking expedition but a cool one none the less: unsupported and unassisted solo ski expedition to the South Pole by Finnish Vesa Luomala. Vesa is in... Antarctica skiing 1100km from Hercules Inlet to the Pole. When Vesa reaches the Pole, he will be the first Finnish to do so solo and also complete the longest solo expedition by a Finn.

Daniel and Vesa had been out there, never in sight but always "together." The great Finnish Nordic skier, Vesa Luomala, had just been the first Finn to *ski* from the coast to the South Pole, solo, unassisted, no resupplies. Daniel observed that Vesa had skied from coast to Pole almost as fast as Daniel had cycled from coast to Pole, but the principle of doing an extraordinary feat first was the same in both cases.

Vesa and Daniel embraced and smiled at each other. It had been nearly two months since they had met at the base camp before their expedition. They had both been alone for over 50 days and yet a connection had formed. In all the electronic communications the explorers had shared with their supportive loved ones, Daniel's wife, Media, and Vesa's girlfriend had found out about each other and shared information about their explorers. Daniel recalls, "When Vesa arrived, I was surprised that he knew all about how my expedition had gone from information he had obtained through his calls to his girlfriend."

Jaakko concluded:

As fat bikes have evolved the idea of pedaling to the South Pole has gained popularity during the recent years. Eric Larsen gave it a try the last season but turned back as the going was too slow (my hat is off for trying and finishing in good style). Now American Daniel Burton is giving it a go on his South Pole Epic trying to cycle from Hercules Inlet to the Pole with resupplies on the way. Another contender for the "first" is Spanish Juan Menéndez Grandos (sic) who hopes to complete the journey without resupplies. This autumn Huan (sic) crossed Greenland with guided Norwegian group cycling some parts and mostly pulling his bike in a pulka. This raises the question how much you have to cycle to say you've cycled to the South Pole? All the way? 90%? 50%? 10%? I don't know but it's interesting to see what the fat bikes can get you.

Daniel cared about the skiing bike tow-er who claimed Daniel's record. "I've heard that Juan is out of food, so I'm asking that everyone keep him in their prayers."

After a flight back to the base camp on Union Glacier, the seasoned Antarctica explorers welcomed Daniel. They kept track of all the expeditions and so could check off Daniel Burton, safely in and off his bike. These ice burned heroes sat with Dan, questioning him with keen interest. Gradually, Daniel came in from the alien reality to his new social reality. He began to hear people and hear himself. He could connect with the people who earnestly sought to communicate with him. "I was interesting to them now, *after* the expedition," he realized. He had paid his dues and joined the South Pole Adventure Club. "Now I'm one of them, an extreme adventurer," Daniel thought to himself, but he didn't say that out loud.

Before Daniel started out on his expedition he would have silently inserted himself into technical discussions. He was an outsider and not really one of the real explorers. Now that he had finished his expedition, he was one of them and they accepted him. They were curious about the details of the expedition. "How did you deal with the soft snow? What was it like biking in a white out? How did the bike handle the sastrugi? How much could you pedal, and how much did you have to push? The extreme explorer adventurers (of which he was now one) listened with astonishment as the latest record holder, *the* Daniel Burton, detailed the expedition.

The technical discussions were wonderful. Daniel was engaged. Everybody was intensely curious about everybody else's experience and technique. But underneath it all, for Daniel, the questions behind the questions were, "How did I get to the South Pole? How did I wind up here? When did the expedition start? Was it when I met Eric Larsen, the professional, career, extreme explorer adventurer, and only one to have attempted what I just accomplished? Was it discovering that the boy who loved camping and hiking had become a soft, young, computer programmer... who then got laid off? Was it riding my bicycle to church and then finding salvation from weight gain and high cholesterol by riding 100 miles, down an open road? Was it because I somehow genetically inherited the adventurous spirit of the people from whom I descend?

Child of explorers

Strange how we inherit things from distant ancestors. Anybody who knew Daniel Burton knew that as a kid, he would wander off on his own and explore. This frequently got him lost and struggling to get back to safety. Daniel would comment on that description of himself by noting that the attraction and the thrill of exploration (of the geographic terrain without and the spiritual terrain within) is "part of who I am."

Daniel was named after an early American forbear who did not sit in the shadow of mountains, but rather ran up and over them. This 18th century American kid would go off for days at a time to hunt and explore and would later insist, "I can't say as ever I was lost, but I was bewildered once for three days." The maiden name of Daniel Burton's mother is Boone. Her father, Daniel's grandfather, was named Daniel Boone. This is because Daniel Burton, formerly chubby software programmer, drew a straight line from the sedentary keystroker to his sixth great grandfather, the great explorer Daniel Boone.

Also, there was some DNA, some genome map that put him in mind of striking out over frozen vastness, seeking a pinpoint goal. This led him to the story of Sir Ernest H. Shackleton, the strangely dominant figure in "the heroic age of Antarctic exploration," who never made it to the South Pole in three tries, one of which was an attempt to *cross* the Antarctic Continent *through* the South Pole. Ironically Shackleton's fame is more remembered in books and films on account of his leadership and endurance, saving the lives of his comrades on desperate expeditions, than Robert Scott, who led the first Antarctic expedition, and Roald Amundsen, who was the first to reach the South Pole.

It is true that Shackleton got his men out of terrible fixes, but a comparison of the biographies of Shackleton, Scott, and Amundsen reveals that their rivalries and competitiveness also got them into those terrible fixes. Scott died out on the ice after having reached the South Pole because his order to have his party met by a resupply party on the return was not carried out. Shackleton tried and tried but never got to the Pole. His government and private backers noted in their reports of his expeditions that his preparations were designed to beat the others rather than to ensure safe success. Only Amundsen had the plan, the support, and the judgment to get his men all the way in and all the way back out and even Amundsen in the emotional stress of the climactic rush to the Pole so humiliated a member of his expedition (who was a renowned explorer in his own right and, therefore, a rival for glory) that the man, upon returning home to Norway, committed suicide.

Ernest Shackleton intended to be the first to reach the North Pole, but he was beaten by Commander Robert Peary of the U.S. Navy, who *thought* he was at the North Pole on April 6, 1909 only to find out later that Dr. Frederick Cook was *sure* he was at the pole in 1908. In speaking with the very young National Geographic Society, Ernest Shackleton explained that there was now no point for him in a North Pole quest and so he set off for Antarctica and the South Pole. His *Discovery* expedition was hastily assembled so he could beat the methodical and professional Norwegian team of Roald Amundsen and Scott's British team. They got to the South Pole. He almost got to the Pole.

Unable to tolerate that defeat, Shackleton created the ultimate polar expedition, his Transantarctic Expedition…a trek from one side of the Antarctic continent to the other *through* the South Pole, 1100 miles on foot and by dog sled. In his sailing ship, the *Endurance,* Shackleton got near the Antarctic coast on the Weddell Sea where he planned to set off for the Pole, but the pack ice closed in on the ship and crushed it. The party had to winter on the drifting ice and ended up sailing across the most dangerous seas in the world in small open boats to reach land and rescue, having killed their beloved sled dogs, but saved their own lives. Shackleton's heroic high point came when he left his men on Elephant Island, *rowed* to South Georgia Island, got help from a *Norwegian* whaling station (bitter irony) and sailed back to rescue all twenty-two members of his expedition. *Moral: Mankind's wilderness expeditions must not be about glory and reward, but about achievement and knowledge. Plan humbly. Succeed greatly.* Sir Ernest Shackleton, it turns out, is Daniel Burton's eighth cousin, just enough like Daniel to be inspiration, not enough like Daniel to be a bad example.

Daniel's and Vesa's expeditions were coming in from the pole just as everybody was shutting down the Union Glacier base camp for the winter. Like a spirit observing the alien scene, Daniel still blogged out his observations.

When we get back to Union Glacier they are in the process of taking down the base camp. It feels like we are in a ghost town.

As Daniel Burton moved about, arranging his return home, the staff of the Union Glacier camp facilities that had, among their many duties, the responsibility to monitor these expeditions out on the ice, were at times startled to see him, a gentlemanly, older man coming up behind them to ask for help. All of them started off by asking the same question. In the motion picture, *Lawrence of Arabia*, Lawrence comes into Egypt out of the Sinai desert after horrible adventures and beholds the Suez Canal. On the other side of the canal, a British soldier on a motorcycle stops and peers at Lawrence. When Alice chases the White Rabbit down the tunnel under the tree, the Cheshire cat studies Alice. The people of ALE at South Pole Station, the British motorcycle soldier and the White Rabbit all ask the same question, "Who are you?"

Union Glacier base camp

An Unremarkable but Admirable Life

Daniel Burton lived an unremarkable but admirable life on the shores of Utah Lake, in Utah County, in the state of Utah. He was born in Corvallis, Oregon. With a strange sense of humor he likes to say, "When I was three months old my family moved to Alaska, but I found them anyway." The Burton family lived in Alaska until Daniel was three and then moved to Utah.

Daniel Burton remembers, "When I was young my family would go hiking in the High Uintas of Utah. One trip I remember, I had what I thought was a heavy backpack. I was just a little kid so it probably only had my sleeping bag in it. I remember hiking for what seemed like a long distance, in reality it was only a few miles. When I took off my pack it gave me the feeling of weightlessness. Running seemed like being an astronaut bounding across the surface of the moon."

Like Daniel Boone, Daniel liked to roam, but unlike Daniel Boone, Daniel frequently would get lost. "When I was about 4 or 5 years of age my family went on a camping and fishing trip to Joe's Valley Reservoir. My father was fishing on a steep part of the reservoir shore. I guess I was being rambunctious, as kids tend to be, and so my father, not wanting me to get lost, told me to sit on a boulder and to not get off of it for any reason. I was sitting on the boulder when it rolled over and dropped into the lake. The water dropped off very deeply at the shore and so I was dumped into super cold, deep water. I remember I kept coming up for air and then sinking back under. My dad jumped in, and even though he isn't a great swimmer, swam out and rescued me."

His father continues the story, "It was summer and the water level in the reservoir had dropped, exposing a muddy shore line dotted with a few large rocks. I was fishing on a steep part of the Reservoir near a point It was hard to keep track of Daniel and fish too, so after a while I sat him on one of the large rocks near the reservoir and told him not to get off for any reason.

"I got engrossed in fishing and wasn't paying any attention to Danny. All of a sudden my pregnant wife yelled that Danny had fallen into the water. I looked up and the rock that Danny had been sitting on had slid down the steep muddy slope, landing several yards out into the water. The momentum of the slide had launched Danny several yards further and he was getting farther from the shore by the moment.

"I was 50 or so yards from Danny and not really dressed for swimming. I had on heavy hiking boots, Levi pants, a fishing jacket, a fishing creel and pockets full of everything a fisherman wants while fishing. I dropped my fishing pole and ran as fast as I could to the shore near Danny. At this time, he was yelling bloody murder and in spite of his best efforts to stay afloat, going under.

"I jumped in the water, swam out to him the best I could and got him to the surface. He was in a state of panic and grabbed on to me trying to climb up into my arms. I couldn't swim with him dressed as I was. I threw him as far as I could toward the shore which in turn pushed me away from the shore. I then swam over to him and repeated the process until I got close enough to the shore to carry him to his frantic mother. In Google satellite images you can still see the large rock Danny rode into the water."

When Daniel publicized his intentions to bike to the South Pole he received a lot of criticism from people like Mike Curiak. Mike is an inductee in the Mountain Bike Hall of Fame. His nomination says,

> When discussing modern endurance mountain bike racing, you can't have a conversation without the name of Mike Curiak popping up somewhere along the way. Mike has not only performed at the highest level in this sport, he has led the way in defining its very nature, as well as documented its emerging history in the media.
>
> As race mileages increased, Mike's race results improved dramatically. In the relatively short 100 mile or 24 hour races, Mike had infrequent success, but the longer distances seemed to inspire him to ride at a level beyond what many (including Mike!) thought possible. His accolades include winning and setting course records at the most difficult and challenging races yet known: Iditasport Impossible (1,100 miles), Iditarod Trail Invitational (350 and 1,100 miles), Grand Loop Race (340 miles) Great Divide Race (2500 miles), and Kokopelli Trail Race (142 miles).

Mike's races on the snowy, icy, sled dog route of the Iditarod made him famous, and at one time he had aspirations of riding a bike to the South Pole. On the Mountain Bike Review Forum, mtbr.com, Mike told Daniel,

> My $.02 is that you are doing yourself (and those that would attempt it in the future) an enormous disservice by going from "nothing" to Antarctica. In other words, please, for your own good if no one else's, go somewhere else (Alaska, Norway, Greenland, NWT, wherever) and do a

14

big, scary, push-your-limits shakedown ride (or three, or more) before moving forward on "The Big One". The point is to do your learning in a safer place, biting off bigger and bigger chunks before committing to something that, quite frankly, you do not and cannot grasp yet.

This did not dissuade Daniel. It seems he has a knack for adventuring too far, and not being afraid of getting in over his head. He tells the story, "Even though my dad isn't a good swimmer, he is a good scuba diver. He just doesn't know how to swim without fins. One time we were at some lake in Idaho. My dad and uncle were out scuba diving, and we kids were playing in the water. My dad and uncle warned us not to go out too far because there was a big drop off. Of course, while they were out scuba diving, I ended up going out too far and stepping off of the drop off. I was again bobbing up and down in the water, and my dad happened to return from his diving trip just in time to save me."

Was Daniel being foolish for going from nothing to Antarctica? Was he getting in over his head? Or is it possible that other events in his life had taught him the skills needed to survive in the world's ultimate wilderness? Daniel's wilderness "training" started at a young age.

"My dad loves to fish, so we would go on hiking and fishing trips a lot. A lot of times while we would be getting ready to go on a hiking trip my brother Mike and I (the two kids that did most of the hiking trips with my dad) would be trying to keep our packs as light as possible. Our dad would tell us we should take a pad to sleep on. We would tell him we could deal with the hard ground. We would want to leave the fishing poles behind. We wanted our packs to be as light as possible. For Mike and me, fishing wasn't necessary, but my dad could not understand how you could go hiking and not fishing."

Daniel also explored out of the safe zone intellectually. "I wasn't always the best student. In second grade our teacher would give us math assignments. There were dozens of three digit addition problems like 294+323. I noticed at the bottom of the page there were the answers in code. It would have "1. sfgo 2. ratnm." For some reason I figured if the teacher saw me putting in random answers I would get in trouble, so, until recess, I solved problems and worked on deciphering the code. In the first problem I saw that if the answer was 8532, then I would know "s" was an "8," "f" was a "5," "g" was a "3," and "o" was a "2." After deciphering what letter went with what number, I could then just fill in the answers using the code. But I would work slowly so I didn't have to put too much effort into figuring out the code, because really I was just delaying until the teacher would leave, and I could fill in the answers with random numbers.

"The strange thing when I look back at this is that somehow I thought if the teacher saw me putting random numbers in I would get in trouble, but I can't understand why I thought she would be able to tell I was just making up random numbers.

"The teacher would take everyone out that had finished the assignment and everyone else had to finish before they could leave. After the teacher left, I would fill in random numbers and turn in the assignment. I never have been good at basic arithmetic. However, in the 6th grade they had a program where they tested and figured out your math ability. Then you would work through a set of cards at your own rate. I started out that year doing third grade math, but being able to go at my own rate I finished the year doing 7th and 8th grade math."

His math journey continued into junior high school. "Because of a 50 mile wilderness hiking trip, I missed the first couple of days of junior high. That first day they gave a math test that determined which math class I would be in. The teacher, Mr. Loveless, was really upset that I had missed school for a hiking trip and refused to let me take the test to see if I could be in a higher math class. He was going over some math that was no different than what we learned years ago in grade school. I complained to someone sitting next to me that this was stupid math that I already knew. Mr. Loveless heard, but didn't hear exactly who had said it. He took a yardstick and walked down the row between the chairs and smacked everyone in the head with the yardstick. When I went home I told my mother. She called the school and insisted that they give me the math test to determine which math class I belonged in [The author, Tip, asks, 'but not that Mr. Loveless stop hitting her son with a yardstick?' 'No,' Dan reflects, 'I think in my day, if you acted up in school, then you deserved to be disciplined')." Dan explained the outcome, "I got moved into the advanced math class. When I went to college I passed all the math classes needed for a math minor, yet I still do not know my multiplication tables, and use my fingers to add."

Daniel's father was a college professor, which meant that he would have a lot of vacation time in the summers and would spend that time with his sons hunting and fishing in the outdoors. "My dad also loved to hunt. When I was old enough to carry a rifle, I would go deer hunting with him. I think maybe my poor eye sight made it so I was not a good hunter. I never was able to find a deer that I could tell was a buck so I never ended up shooting a deer. I also did a lot of bow hunting with my dad. When I started I got a really cool compound bow. Compound bows were new back then. It was everything I could do to pull the string back on the bow. When I would practice shooting the bow, I would only use one arrow because I only had the strength to pull the string back one time. But after walking out to the target and getting the arrow and then going back to the bow, my arm would recover enough that I could do it again.

"I was never a good hunter, but, like fishing, I went hunting not for the hunt but just to be outdoors. After I became an adult, I quit hunting because I was afraid that I might actually get a deer, and then I'd have to gut it and take care of it, and I really had no interest in cleaning out a deer. I grew up spending my summers in the outdoors with my father, and then as a father I would take my son on extended outings in Utah's High Uintas Wilderness Area."

This is Daniel Burton's attempt to express the image of his life as an explorer, as a seeker, an investigator and a pilgrim into a new world of understanding, up to a new plateau of knowledge and mastery of environment …mastery of self.

O Pioneers!

Daniel has studied the lives of his own pioneer ancestors. "We'll never really understand… What did they go through? What did they seek? How did they prepare?"

Daniel Burton is descended from Willard Richards, who was with Joseph Smith in Carthage Jail in Illinois when Joseph and his brother, Hyrum, were killed by an angry mob. Later, Willard Richards would be with his cousin, Brigham Young, in the pioneer company of The Church of Jesus Christ of Latter-day Saints that, in the summer of 1847, made the "Mormon Trail" to the Valley of the Great Salt Lake. After helping Cousin Brigham to establish the settlement which today is called Salt Lake City, Willard turned around and got back to Winter Quarters, Nebraska so he could lead the 1848 "Willard Richards Company" of Mormon pioneers west along the trail he helped open up to the city "in the tops of the mountains."

Daniel is also descended from Lot Smith, called "the Horseman" by his friend, Orrin Porter Rockwell. Lot Smith was a frontier scout, rancher, and founder of the Mormon colony of Tuba City, Arizona. As a very young man, Lot Smith had marched with the Mormon Battalion from Fort Leavenworth, Kansas to San Diego, California to fight for the United States in the Mexican War that was over by the time they got there. Ten years later, Lot became a leader in the "Nauvoo Legion" that harassed and delayed the advance of "Johnston's Army" that had the mission of "punishing" the Saints for supposed rebellion against the U.S. The Deseret News newspaper reports,

"Lot Smith encountered an Army supply train here on Oct. 2, 1857. Amid his threats, the train promised to return east to avoid being burned. But as soon as Smith's militia was out of sight, the supply train turned west again to try to join the infantry and find protection.

After that, Smith decided to burn wagon trains whenever he had the chance—and burned 50 wagons in two detachments on Oct. 3. The next day he burned another unprotected train, after Smith and the wagon master had a short, classic conversation. "(I asked) him to get all of his men and their private property as quickly as possible out of the wagons for I meant to put a little fire to them.

"He [the wagon master] exclaimed, 'For God's sake, don't burn the trains.' I said it was for his sake that I meant to burn them."

—Captain Lot Smith, Mormon militia

The raids on the Army's horses and mules as well as their cattle motivated General Albert Sydney Johnston to negotiate a peace accord with Brigham Young.

Daniel Burton (like Daniel Boone and the other pioneer ancestors) was the existential explorer. Often, when he would be lost and alone in the woods, he would contemplate an idea that one day would be made into a motion picture, *The Truman Show*. Daniel wondered, "Is it possible that everything is fake? Is it possible that everything is just a big stage and everyone around is just an actor and scenes set up for me and that nothing is real?" What did Shakespeare have Jaque say in *As You Like It*? "All the world's a stage and all the men and women in it merely players."

He had pondered these thoughts since he was very young, as young as he could remember. *The Truman Show* came out when he was an adult (1998). After watching the show he was shocked to learn that feeling you are just on a stage, that you were like Truman, was uncommon.

Daniel found his way in life better than many youths, but not without stress and uncertainty. Daniel embraced his identity as a Latter-day Saint, a "Mormon," but within that set of circumstances he still had to ask: What am I supposed to be? Where am I supposed to go? Daniel remembers going through something most of us feared at one time. "I remember when I was young and we would go out to play a game like baseball or football, or really any game, the results were always the same. We would all gather in a group and then the two team captains would take turns picking people to be on their team. No matter how good I thought I was at a game, I was always the last one picked to be on a team."

But Daniel was chosen for other things. When he was in 7th or 8th grade, near the end of those same 70s, Daniel had started using punch cards to program computers. These room filling machines were unlike the personal computers that followed them or the laptops of yesterday or the smart phone-think pad-tablets of today. Daniel remembers, "Computer programming was easy for me, and when I was in high school a couple of people in my neighborhood were taking a computer programming class at BYU. They asked me for help with their programs, and I ended up doing the programming for them. It was easy for me to write the programs, but I wasn't very good at teaching them how to program. Of course, I hung out with the computer geeks in high school."

In 1982, Daniel graduated from Mountain View High school in the shadow of Mount Timpanogos, which dominates the line of mountains along the Wasatch Front. He inherited the strength of the hills as he served an LDS mission in Pittsburgh, Pennsylvania. He then created a solid career in computer science in Utah's cyber crossroads of the West.

Mormons (and other explorers) write in their journals

Daniel chronicled his life as a journal keeper, not always devout, but to accomplish his purpose of self-analysis, goal setting, and project planning. "I went to BYU (Brigham Young University, in Provo, Utah) for one year before going on an LDS mission to Pittsburgh, PA. I was majoring in Electrical Engineering and had all of the math classes required for an EE major completed before going on my mission. I started working for WordPerfect the day I got home from my mission (Do we all remember the beautiful WordPerfect? It was a Utah company built by Mormon cyber-pioneers that launched the now huge Utah technology industry. Think Oracle and Micron and Novell). Daniel continued, "Apparently, some of the people at WordPerfect thought I was a child prodigy. It turns out that one of the executives at WordPerfect was one of the BYU students for whom I had done homework.

"I ended up dropping out of college to work full time for WordPerfect and advanced to a well paid position. Eventually, WordPerfect was bought out by Novell and so I ended up being a Novell employee. When I was at Novell, I started doing some extra work of my own on the side. I created an internet file sharing solution and ended up getting two software patents for my inventions. The work I did ended up getting combined with the work of a software team to create an internet file sharing feature in *NetWare*."

By his late 30s, Daniel Burton had a beautiful family. Daniel first met Media Thomas in their seventh grade French class. Neither one of them knew anything about Jason and his Argonauts or the tale of Medea. They became good friends during high school when they were in the same Physics and Calculus classes. Daniel dated Media during his first year at BYU before leaving on an LDS mission, but Media didn't exactly "wait" for Daniel during his two year mission. They weren't that far along in their relationship. In fact, she wrote Daniel a "Dear John" letter, but ended up not sending it. She still has that Dear John letter as an unusual memento of over 30 years of courtship and marriage...which has also produced four great kids.

But something was very wrong with this oh, so very right family portrait. Daniel was a typical American in bad ways as well as good. His career as a Novell programmer made him prosperous, but also made him overweight, pre-diabetic, and with heart-unhealthy high cholesterol. He had the feeling that he would die of this unhealthy lifestyle. He could not afford a lethal attitude of not caring, not believing, not being willing to set goals and reach them with no thought of the possibility of failure. In fact, his mother would eventually die of that constellation of heart disease issues (like millions of Americans) and catalyze Daniel's decision to go for it in Antarctica. His expedition would not be about glory and reputation (Shackleton) but rather about example and showcasing the great cause (Amundsen) of health, wellness, and fitness. As a computer programmer, Daniel was getting chubbier and chubbier, and his cholesterol was rising. These mundane threats could cost him his beautiful life. Daniel began to think deeply about the purpose of his life. He entered what we too frivolously call a midlife crisis.

Daniel's lessons learned: "I really panicked when I got the cholesterol test back. I was scared that I would die. Even though intellectually I knew it was not going to kill me immediately, it was almost as if I expected it would. I figured it could happen any day. For a couple of months I was eating almost nothing. I would come home from work starving, and go through all the food in the house. We had a lot of food storage so there was a lot for me to look through. I would go through all of it looking at the labels." Sugar, starch, bad fats, trans fats—almost everything the typical American and even the typical Mormon eats will make you fat or raise your cholesterol. Daniel continues, "I could not get myself to eat it. About the only thing I could get myself to eat was oatmeal. And I could not bear the thought of adding milk or sugar to the oatmeal. I also started eating Cheerios. I have always hated Cheerios, but for some reason at this point in my life I actually liked them. Again, I would eat them with no sugar, but I was able to get myself to use nonfat milk. I had started biking, and my exercise and very little food made me drop about 30 pounds quite quickly, though probably this was not a healthy way to do it. However, after my weight got down to a little over 150, my cholesterol numbers returned to normal and my blood pressure numbers leveled off, so I started eating again. I have tried to be better about what I eat since then, and I have kept up the biking."

As Daniel said it in his journal,

> All my years as a computer programmer left me about 30 pounds overweight, not good but actually not abnormally heavy.

Tip says, "We hear the doctors saying, *don't make excuses, Dan. Thirty pounds is absolutely not healthy.*"

Daniel knew it was not healthy to mix his "age appropriate" body fat percentage and genetically stubborn high cholesterol. Daniel recounts,

> It was after the particularly distressing cholesterol test I really got into mountain biking. Before long I was doing century[1] mountain and road bike rides.

---

[1] A "century" is a one hundred mile bicycle race or rally, maybe over paved roads, but, more to Daniel's purpose, maybe off road and up into the mountains.

I figured this had saved my life, and when I got laid off at Novell I opened a bike store to help others get into cycling.

The computer genius without a degree but with technology patents had been gobbled up and laid off by that same employer…21st century tech bubble bursting. Now what? Daniel was living on the west side of Utah Lake at the foot of the Oquirrh Mountains, which make the western side of Utah Valley. He had biked around the lake to commute to his job in Provo on the eastern side at the foot of the Wasatch Mountains. Now he observed the latest in outdoor exercise and adventure…mountain biking…cool. For high cholesterol, high blood sugar and excess weight, take two to three bicycle rides per day—cycle 100 miles around the lake from home in Eagle Mountain to work in Provo, and a mountain bike ride for lunch. Repeat daily. His morning and evening commute around Utah Lake was a starting point for his endurance preparation.

Daniel explains his conversion to the bike culture. "There was a group of people that were into biking at Novell, and they were inviting me to go

White Rim in Canyonlands

biking with them. Then my son's scout group decided to do the White Rim in Canyonlands. I volunteered to be one of the parents going on the trip. I think the other people from church were surprised because they didn't think I was the type to go on a three day biking and camping trip. Juan Carlos Luciani, one of my work friends, helped me pick out a bike for the White Rim trip, and I went and did the 100 mile three day mountain biking trip. When I got through with that trip, I started riding bikes with the people at Novell. We rode almost every day.

"Then one day my bishop, Mike Boyd, who was a serious biker and the one that put together the White Rim scout trip, invited me to do a 100 mile road bike ride. I told him I didn't own a road bike. His response, 'Go buy one.' So I bought a road bike, took it to work and showed the guys at work my new bike. We took turns riding it around the halls. Then a couple of days later, without ever having really ridden a road bike before, we set off on my first 100 mile (112 actually) bike ride. After I opened my bike store I started using that route for the "Pony Express Century"[2] which I have been running as an organized century for six years.

The mountains and valleys of Utah are pocked with successful and failed mines for gold, lead, zinc, tin, iron and coal, as well as one of the largest open pit copper mines in the world. Every spine of mountains has canyons reaching deep into the ridge line leading the way to hidden mines and old, deserted mining towns. These mountains and their canyons became the unofficial cross country courses for the exploding mountain bike community of extreme athletes and local explorers. The town of Eagle Mountain, where Daniel Burton lives, has embraced the mountain bike culture and built a mountain bike specific park with trails, jumps and areas to develop mountain biking skills. That is why Daniel's store, Epic Biking, is in a mall complex at the base of Lake Mountain in

---

[2] Utah History

The route of the Pony Express ran from Salt Lake City out west to the Jordan River and then south to Saratoga Springs, thence westward past Eagle Mountain to Cedar Fort and on into Utah's Western Desert to Pony Express stations at Callao and Simpson Springs. The Pony Express went across Nevada, over the Sierra Nevada Mountains into California and reached its western terminus at Sacramento, California. Daniel Burton led as many cyclists as would sign up for a ride on a hundred mile bike ride that incorporated the route of the Pony Express.

what used to be the rapidly growing crossroads hamlet called Saratoga Springs along the historic Pony Express Trail.

Daniel discovered Slate Canyon (which is east of Novell in Provo) and, joined by the cyclists from Novell, started pushing higher and higher up the canyon on their lunchtime rides. "I think very few people bike up that canyon. It was a steep, rocky, dirt road. We would ride up on most days during lunch."

Also east of Novell is the "Y" on the side of the mountain. The trail up to the Y is a steady, steep climb. The challenge was to see if you could make it all the way to the top of the Y without putting a foot down. Daniel figures, "Slate Canyon and the Y trail taught me how to recover from a hard effort yet continue to climb." Daniel would ride mountain bikes with the group to test their legs up, up the twisting trail through the rocks in the mountain canyons. This strengthened his legs for his eventual epic adventure to the South Pole.

All of this mountain biking guru gang leadership, combined with the urge to explore both new terrain and also new bicycle technology led Daniel Burton to the fateful step.

From the Journal of Daniel Burton:

June 26, 2001

Discovered a new game today called geocaching. We took an old tin can and put a logbook and some old happy meal toys and stashed it in an old car in the gully by where some train tracks used to go across. The pilings are still there and I guess if you know what you're looking at you can still see the old railroad grade. Then, using a GPS, we noted the location (40° 22.19′ N 111°59.30′ W) and entered the information about our cache on the Internet. Then others can try to locate it.

[Our four children] Stephan, Carissa, Danae, Myron and I also went and found a cache someone else had created. It was down by the Jordan River at 40 24.21 111 53.99. I think the kids had fun doing it. They did complain about all the walking they did, but I think it was good for them. Myron took a toy car and a Tarzan from the cache. We left a happy meal toy and a drink. Carissa wanted to leave the drink because she got so hot and thirsty while we were hiding our cache.

Journal:

June 27, 2001

Stephan and Carissa have been doing space camp this summer. Stephan is excited because he has been doing this the last couple years and now has enough "points" that he gets an admiral rank, which means he gets to choose what he does in the simulators.

Carissa has a lower rank so she has fewer options by the time she gets to choose. She has been choosing radar operator. I guess she was taking it quite seriously because she was quite worried about the Borg. I think a lot of why she likes space camp is because Stephan likes it. She really looks up to Stephan.

Journal:

7 December 2001

Today Media, Carissa, and I started a seven-day cruise of the Caribbean. We flew to Puerto Rico and boarded the Celebrity Galaxy.

Stephan and Danae each had a chance to have a special vacation. Stephan went to Germany and France and Danae went to Washington DC. Anyway, we set sail tonight. Carissa says the cruise is not what she expected. The ship is "way cooler" and the islands are larger than she expected. We had to circle over the San Juan airport three or four times waiting for the rain to die down enough to land.

IAH Houston Airport 29° 58.97 N 95° 20.09 W

PRRC Puerto Rico dock 18° 27.49N 66° 05.81W

Journal:

10 December 2001 13° 6.5 N 59° 39.83 W

We are just pulling into Barbados. Last time, this was our favorite island. Media says she thinks she liked St. Kitts better than what she remembers of Barbados. We went to church yesterday in St. Kitts. The island has a small population and doesn't seem too overrun by tourists. However, we didn't get to see much because we had so little time in port and spent most of it in church. At dinner last night there was a lady at the table next to ours who was telling the waiter that she was related to Daniel Boone. When I heard this I turned around and started talking to her. She is from Kentucky and is a descendent of Sarah Boone, Daniel's sister. What is the lady's name? Melody Mc???

Journal:

9 April 2002

Myron has been asking if he could get a CD-ROM game for the computer. He told me that if we bought it he would do better in school next year. I didn't realize that it was something the school was doing as some fundraiser. This morning when he was getting ready for school, Media started looking for his coat. She couldn't find it, so she decided to check Myron's backpack. He told her it wasn't in there and that she didn't need to look. When she looked inside against Myron's protests she found the envelope from school full of every bit of money Myron could find, including some French and Italian coins. The CD-ROM game was hidden in his room and he was going to use the coins he found to pay for it. Media made him return the CD-ROM. It was cute to see a little six-year-old try to take matters into his own hands to get the game.

Journal:

28 August 2002

Myron came in from playing outside and asked for a sharp knife. When we asked what for he said so he could cut himself. He said he wanted to make a scar. It took me a while to figure out why. He wanted a scar on his forehead so everyone would know that he really is Harry Potter. So I took a marker and drew a scar on his forehead.

There is something in the Bible about when ye have seen the son, ye have seen the father.

Epic Biking

So Daniel did the thing dreaded by the wife of a dreamer, he quit his job… well, not quit exactly. He had been laid off, but he left his career, his safe path. Daniel opened "Epic Biking," a specialty bicycle shop in Saratoga Springs, Utah. Epic Biking was supposed to sell a few bikes and get more people into cycling while hopefully providing an income for the Burton family of six with its four kids. It became, however, a club, a band of brothers and sisters who gathered around Daniel to learn the potential of the bike for self-development.

Daniel had realized the true principle, which is that you won't exercise in an activity you don't love. Daniel got on a bike and loved it. He discovered that he loved his achievements as an extreme athlete. He dedicated himself to cycling and committed to Epic Biking. It was there that he formed his intention to land on the coast of Antarctica in the austral summer and pedal all the way to the South Pole.

Journal:

23 July 2009

We have been doing better at the bike store than I expected this week. Last year the week of the 24th was dead.[3]

This year it has been dead most of July and picked up this week. However, I'm afraid I am not going to make it. I have to pay all the invoices for stuff I bought this month and rent and I expect I will

---

[3] In Utah, and other places with large Mormon communities, the 24th of July is "Pioneer Day," the day in 1847 when Brigham Young—and Daniel Burton's ancestor, Willard Richards—led the first company of pioneers into Salt Lake Valley

end the month with no money saved up. I just don't know how I will be able to place the required enrollment orders for the 2010 bikes. I've been trying to figure out an additional business I could run in my space to help pay the rent, especially during the winter months. I thought I'd sell baked treats and bread, rolls etc. It could work if Media would make the goods, but she doesn't want to do that. I think it is a great idea, but it won't work without Media. Myron wants to open a Lego store, but I don't think we could do that. I am considering selling board games, but not sure if doing so will make the store seem like it is not a serious bike store and end up hurting the bike business. I don't know, but I have to do something or it will be over soon.

Overlooking Utah Valley

Epic Biking Needs a South Pole Epic

Planning and preparation

Daniel Burton had a revelation. He had a cause: cycling to save lives with health, wellness, and fitness. The cause had a headquarters: Epic Biking. The headquarters needed to plan an expedition to draw attention to the cause.

Daniel started with a daydream.

OK, I've got a plan for a new adventure. I'm not quite ready to make it public yet, but I can't contain myself, so I have to say something without really saying anything. No big deal though, because I doubt anyone is reading this blog since I haven't been posting anything to it for a long time. I'm really excited about my project, but when I talk to people about it the conversation goes something like this:

Me: "I have this great idea…" and I bore him with my plan.

Person who doesn't really want to hear me babble about the idea: "That just sounds miserable."

Me: "From everything I read it IS!"

Person: "Being miserable for two months? Why would you do it?"[4]

"Because… ah… think how cool it would be! I could be the first! I would be in Wikipedia!"

But then I think being in Wikipedia and in the record books really isn't that important to me. However, I am trying to convince people that this would be a good idea, and so I used this as an excuse to do it.

My imaginary dialogue partners says, "Look, I can add you to Wikipedia right now if you would like."

---

[4] Sir Ranulph Fiennes said, "Those that ask the question will never understand the answer. Those that understand the answer will never ask the question." Yet, the question is unavoidable. Maybe the answer is that I am like Mr. Toad in *The Wind in the Willows:* I was infected with a mania and there was no stopping it. All I talked about, all I thought about, all I wanted to do was bike to the South Pole. It was irrational, but I could not overcome the mania. Other reasons to do this — to help people be more physically active, or to fight high cholesterol and heart disease — are real, but to some extent merely an excuse for my mania.

29

"I could be in the *Guinness Book of World Records!*"

"Yeah, if you don't die first."

"But, but, it would be so awesome!"

Still blogging out his brainstorm, Daniel wrote,

So, do I really have what it takes to do this? I think yes! There is a company[5] that helps with the logistics of this kind of project. I am in contact with them to see how to turn the dream to a real plan. After I get that figured out then I can publicly release what I want to do.

Switching to the *Journal* for the more intimate admissions, Daniel wrote,

Journal — 5 March 2013:

The last five and a half years have been very difficult as I tried to get my bike store going. I have really lost a lot that should've been written down in a journal. However, my new project requires that I keep a journal. I'm going to attempt to be the first person to bike to the South Pole. I've been keeping a blog that is documenting the expedition, but I think there are things I should record but that shouldn't be published on the public blog. But there are also things that should be written both in my journal and in my public blog. I have a lot of people ask me what you do to train for this expedition. Physically I just need to keep my normal routine of exercise every day. I think I'm in good enough shape physically to complete the trip, but there are other things I need to train for doing this expedition and one of them is to write in the journal. I will want a good written log of the trip and I need a good record of what I'm doing leading up to the trip. Also, I think I need to work on my handwriting, both in having it be easier to read and being able to write faster.

---

[5] Antarctic Logistics and Expeditions, Inc. (ALE) provides to private Antarctic expeditions the air transportation, support, and monitoring of expeditionary progress that they need to go out onto the Antarctic ice, take their shot at their goals and return safely. It turns out that the world renowned ALE, the principal contractor relied on by the U.S. and other governments that control Antarctica, *is a Utah Company from right there in Salt Lake City!*

Eric, son of Lars, descendent of Viking explorers

Daniel had been inspired by Eric Larsen. Like Erik the Red, the great Viking that discovered and settled Greenland, Eric Larsen was a great explorer. In fact, Eric is the first (and, indeed, the only) person to do an expedition to the North Pole, the South Pole, and the top of Mount Everest in one year.

Eric had two things he loved, polar exploring and biking. Also, he had this dream of riding a bike to the South Pole. On a cold December day, he set out from the ice shelf and headed south to Antarctica and towards the South Pole. After about 10 days he said on his blog, "This is probably one of the hardest updates I've ever had to write. Today, I've made the decision to abort the Cycle South expedition - at least the rest of the southerly journey to the pole. Instead, I am heading back to my starting point, Hercules Inlet."

Revelation...Now I know

Daniel Burton had a personal revelation of what he was supposed to do. He would finish what Eric Larsen (and, indeed, Ernest Shackleton) had started *for the existential value of it as an inspiration to inner and outer explorers everywhere.*

Daniel continued to record his evolving plan.

> I have a customer that keeps telling me that he is going to win the lottery and then we will bike to the South Pole. Myron is always trying to come up with Kickstarter projects and so I came up with the idea of funding an expedition on Kickstarter. I looked into what it would take to actually do an expedition to the South Pole and my mania took over and now I can think of nothing else but biking to the South Pole. All my crowd funding attempts failed, so I took out a loan to pay for the expedition.

What wife, Media, said about that is not recorded in the journal.

By February of 2013, Daniel had a vision of his expedition and the vision had a name, *South Pole Epic* springing from his desire to live a life of – thus the store — *Epic Biking!*

EpicSouthPole.BlogSpot.com was launched. The inaugural blog post said,

Fat Bikes.

Last December I decided to get into fat bikes. I saw the "Surly Pugsley" a few years ago when I went to FrostBike, a cycling trade show in Minnesota. So I have known about them for a few years, but never really considered buying or selling them. Then I started getting people asking about them. I'm not sure what all else factored into it but I decided to get some fat bikes that I could rent out and start building a fat bike community. Then I got this crazy idea of biking across Utah Lake for New Year's Day.

Everyone was telling him he was crazy for biking across the frozen lake, but it was not even close to as crazy as what was to come.

Utah Lake

Utah Lake freezes over most winters. When I was a kid I heard stories of people trying to ice skate across the lake, falling in and dying. Still, for some reason I decided to bike across Utah Lake. The last week in December was very cold. Nighttime temperatures were in the teens and the highs didn't get above freezing, so I assumed the lake was frozen but didn't really know. New Year's Day we headed out, and found the lake to be solid. We talked to ice fishermen but we never drilled any holes ourselves, so I don't know how thick the ice was but there were no unfrozen cracks, and it *was* plenty thick the whole way. Since then it has

Biking across Utah Lake

been even colder, so the lake had 30 inches of ice a few weeks later when they cut a hole in the ice to do a polar plunge.

South Pole

After the lake trip we started snow biking every chance we could get. Also, just before Christmas, I started reading the fat bike thread on mtbr.com. Someone posted a story about Eric Larsen attempting to ride a "Moonlander" (the same bikes we have) to the South Pole. I started to read his log, and was a little surprised that, after ten days of biking, he turned around. Wow, what an adventure. I was impressed and I would talk about the trip to just about everyone. Then Mark Pendleton started telling me that when he wins the lottery he is going to do the trip with a full support crew and is going to take me with him. Well, I don't see that happening. Nice dream, but, yeah.

However the bug had been planted, and before long the idea of biking to the South Pole would take over.

I Should Do This!

Daniel continued in his planning journal.

I have to be willing to have the most demanding and difficult experience that I will ever have and still be willing to go on. I have to start early enough that I have at least 60 days to travel. And I need a lighter bike. I would like to do it with a support vehicle. Not nearly as courageous as Eric, but if I could have supplies carried by a vehicle[6] that would improve odds of completing tremendously.

The trip would still be an amazing feat, and it would leave the door open for someone to one up me. If, on the other hand, I need to carry my own supplies in order to make the logistics work, then I think a sled would be better than the panniers. I could be wrong, but I think the sled low to the ground and more aero would be better

---

[6] **Is truck support cheating?** In the early planning Daniel was influenced by a desire to make sure the expedition could be a success. Also, he had recruited a friend, Todd Tueller, for the expedition. Daniel is convinced that it was those influences that made him consider using motorized support, but that deep down in his heart he really wanted to do the real thing—make it a true expedition without motorized support, and on the raw, frozen, ice wilderness.

than weighing the bike down, making it hard to stay on top of sastrugi and catching all the wind.

I talked to Eric about sleds instead of panniers. Eric didn't think it was a good idea because the sleds would be too hard to pull. I decided to take sleds and panniers and that would allow me to move the weight to where it worked best.

When he got there, Daniel blogged, "After a few days of experimenting in Antarctica I learned that the sleds were the better idea." So there it is.

What, pray tell, are *sastrugi*?

Wikipedia says that *sastrugi* is a topographical term used all over the Arctic lands from Scandinavia to Siberia. In Russian, the verb "sastrugai" is a woodworking term meaning to "plane or shave down or rout out (a groove)." And the sastrugi do consist of a lot of grooves cut into the ice. Daniel says, "I tried to get pictures of what they looked like but none of my pictures do a good job of showing what they are like. I have also searched the web for pictures and have not found any good pictures that really show what they are like." Thus the plural noun, sastrugi, means wood shavings or grooves in wood. Scott and Shackleton were the first explorers to explain to the world the sastrugi.

Wikipedia's definition: "**Sastrugi**, or **zastrugi**, are sharp irregular grooves or ridges formed on a snow surface by wind erosion, saltation of snow particles, and deposition, and found in polar and temperate snow regions. They differ from sand dunes in that the ridges are markedly parallel to the prevailing winds. Smaller irregularities of this type are known as ripples (small, ~10 mm high), or wind ridges.

"Larger features are especially troublesome to skiers and snowboarders. Traveling on the irregular surface of sastrugi can be very tiring, and can risk breaking equipment—ripples and waves are often undercut, the surface is hard and unforgiving with constant minor topographic changes between ridge and trough."

What the wives ask: "Why exactly are you risking your life this way?" There has to be enough reason.

Daniel blogged beautifully—21 February 2013

Why?

Why do I want to bike to the South Pole? That is the classic question and the classic answer is because it is there. To do something that hasn't been done before, the ultimate challenge! But... I feel the world is facing an obesity crisis. We live a physically easy life compared to the past. Food is relatively cheap, labor is relatively easy, and entertainment is becoming less and less physical.

We Need to Create a Culture of Activity. Nearly everyone needs to have some kind of exercise program. Going to the gym is great. However, if we don't truly enjoy our exercise we will eventually quit. We need to help people find ways to become active that they will enjoy. For me that is biking.

My Story. I was a computer programmer for 23 years. During that time I spent a lot of time sitting in front of a computer and not getting enough exercise. I had grown up being active. I spent a lot of summers hiking in the High Uintas. However it just got easy to be less and less active. Then I went and got my blood checked. My cholesterol numbers were real bad, my blood pressure was high, and I was a few pounds overweight. I panicked, thinking I might die early. So I got into mountain biking. *It saved my life!* My cholesterol numbers improved to healthy numbers, my blood pressure returned to normal, and I lost the extra weight.

Then I got laid off. My wife says that I went into midlife crisis. I think I just decided I wanted to do something to help others. So I opened a bike store to help others get the health benefits of an active cycling lifestyle. For the past 5 years I have been focused on getting people out on bikes, and have been involved with the American Diabetes Association's "Tour de Cure" each year.

The Problem. OK, I've already stated the problem, but here it is in more detail. There are so many problems facing the world today, but I think returning to a culture of active lifestyles will help with so many of today's issues. Obesity is a huge drain on the economy. Violence and lack of concern for others seems to be on the increase. The number of mass shootings recently is beyond alarming. Returning to activity will increase our health, reduce the drain on the economy being caused by runaway health care cost, and help our mental wellbeing. We need to love one another. Being outdoors having fun with others is a great way to learn to get along and be less selfish.

According to the Center for Disease Control (CDC), 'Research has shown that as weight increases to reach the levels referred to as overweight and obesity, the risks for the following conditions also increase:

- Coronary heart disease

- Type 2 diabetes

- Cancers (endometrial, breast, and colon)

- Hypertension (high blood pressure)

- Dyslipidemia (for example, high total cholesterol or high levels of triglycerides)

- Stroke

- Liver and Gallbladder disease

- Sleep apnea and respiratory problems

- Osteoarthritis (a degeneration of cartilage and its underlying bone within a joint)

- Gynecological problems (abnormal menses, infertility)'

My Cause. My cause is simple.

- First to inspire people to get out and be active. Find an activity that you enjoy and you can do on a regular basis. For me that is biking, so I hope my trip to the South Pole will inspire others to get out and ride a bike.

- Second, I would like to encourage people to donate to the American Diabetes Association, or get involved with some other diabetes, cancer, or other health related foundation. I'll be including information in my blog about opportunities to get involved.

Now I need to hear back from Antarctic Logistics and Expeditions (ALE)[7] and see what the real plan is, get the Kickstarter project launched and train for the Pole.

Journal — 6 November 2013:

I imagine a grand Council in heaven. God says, "The journey you are about to embark on will be more difficult than you can imagine. You will experience pain and sorrow, suffering more than you can comprehend. However, it will be worth it. You will also experience joy and happiness that will be greater than anything you have ever known. The joy and happiness that will come from this journey cannot be had unless you also go through the pain and suffering. It will be the overcoming of the trials that will make the reward in the end worthwhile." We all agreed to this plan. However, once we start the journey we find that even though we believed that this would be more difficult than we would beforehand be able to understand, once we are on the journey we find that we wish we didn't have to have such hard times. The pain and sorrow seems more than we can bear. But, as promised, when the journey is complete, the joy is more than we could imagine and He was right; we could not enjoy the happiness at the end had we not gone through the sorrow to get there.

Later, Daniel testified that this "prophecy" turned out to be 100% correct.

Journal — 11 November 2013:

Life isn't fair. Some people work extremely hard and get paid very little. Others don't work so hard and get paid a lot. Some people are smart or athletically gifted. Others may be weak or have difficulty learning or are otherwise disadvantaged. Kate Leeming and Juan

---

[7] ALE Mission statement from ColdAvenger.com: "ALE reaches Antarctic destinations others don't. They provide the logistic support and safety backup needed for climbing groups to Vinson Massif and Antarctica's highest peaks, expeditions to the South Pole and flights to Antarctica. ALE managers and staff have considerable experience and a strong involvement in Antarctica. We believe in safe and sustainable ... expeditions (where) clients leave Antarctica with a greater understanding and appreciation of its natural values. We encourage a culture of environmental awareness within ALE's staff and contractors... ALE is now the only organization offering expedition support and tours to the interior of Antarctica."

Menéndez Granados have worked hard to be qualified and ready to go to the South Pole by bike. They have far more experience than I do, but I believe I will be the first. I've also worked very hard for this.

My last six years of working incredibly hard with no pay may be the best argument for why I qualify to attempt this, but, in the end, fair or not, I am the one that has the chance to do it this year.

Daniel comments, "When I wrote this, Kate had postponed her expedition because she couldn't get funding, and it didn't look like Juan was going to be able to make his expedition. I was thinking that it wasn't fair to Juan and Kate since they had spent more time than I had working towards this goal."

Looking back on the whole adventure, Daniel would later write, "I think that planning for an Antarctic expedition normally takes more time than this. But I figured I had to do it in the austral summer of 2013/2014 or I would lose my chance. I figured that the only way I could pay for the expedition was if it was something nobody had done before."

Daniel had seen that others would claim great achievement even if they hadn't really done it if someone wasn't there to document what really was done and, just as importantly, what was *not* done.

A critical example of this necessity to do it now when the competition was doing it was Daniel's "race to the Pole" with Juan Menéndez Granados[8], the self-styled greatest mountain biker in all Spain, calling himself *Juan Sin Miedo*... "Juan without fear."

When they met in Chile, Juan told Daniel that "Juan Sin Miedo" was Spanish for "Fearless John," the title of a fairy tale about a boy who goes out to learn what fear is. Juan figured everyone knew the tale, but it seemed nobody in Chile or Antarctica knew of the story. Daniel decided that, "If I had not done it when I did, then Juan could have claimed that his ski trip had been by bike and nobody would have known otherwise." Now, however, there was a witness that had seen the tracks in the snow and knew that Juan's was a ski trip and not a bike trip.

Polar exploration and indeed exploration in general has a history of explorers overstating their accomplishments. Frederick Cook, Robert E.

---

[8] Juan Menéndez Granados is not to be confused with Daniel's hometown friend, Juan Carlos Luciani, who was one of the people that got Dan into biking and one of his early supporters for the Antarctic expedition.

Peary and Admiral Richard Byrd each *claimed* to have made it to the North Pole. History says those claims are false.

When Daniel was brainstorming his concept of the expedition, he had an unusual free association. "I figure as I get closer to the actual expedition I will need to condition my rear end to be able to spend more time for multiple days on a bicycle seat. However, the toughness of sitting in the seat goes away real fast, so it needs to be done closer to the actual expedition."

But first things first.

Right now one of the main things I need to work on for the project is the funding. This trip will cost over $250,000, which is a lot of money for me to raise. I've been working on a sponsor letter that is modeled after a business plan and will give prospective sponsors information on the trip and what levels of sponsorship are available and what benefits they get from being a sponsor. I am working on a Kickstarter project for funding also. Kickstarter is set up so you have a funding goal and you don't get any of the money unless you meet your goal. So I think it is important to set the goal low enough that we hit it, but hopefully we can get much more than the initial goal. I think though we will need to do a lot of fundraising outside Kickstarter.[9]

Mike Karr is going to be making a documentary for the expedition. This will be a key part to successfully fund the expedition. We are planning on shooting a Kickstarter project video this week and then we can also use that video to try and get sponsors outside of Kickstarter.

Talking with a guide from Antarctic Logistics and Expeditions (the famous ALE), his guess on the cost paid to ALE will be $280,000. So I think we need to aim for $500,000 and if we come short of that then

---

[9] As time went on, my plans would change. I started with the most expensive and least adventurous plan, but high costs, and an inner desire to experience a true expedition slowly modified the plan to where I was biking alone.

we can still make the expedition happen. It feels like the fundraising will be as difficult[10]—but in a different way—as the trip itself.

Daniel's planning Journal went on,

> I'm trying to think of all the companies we could talk to about being sponsors.... Garmin because we would promote their GPS, or maybe a different GPS manufacturer, maybe Timex.

Later Daniel would admit, "One of the offbeat sponsor ideas I had was Mars candy bars. I could promote Snickers candy bars because they could be an excellent calorie source for the trip. But none of these ideas worked."

Daniel recorded,

> I've also been training for an ironman triathlon but it is so expensive to pay the entrance fees and so I'm not sure I will ever do it. I think I could have a chance to win the Icebreaker Tri at the end of this month and I have been working on running faster to be able to win. But I need to be able to pay the store's bills, and even the entry fee for local triathlons is just too much for someone with no income.

Journal — 12 March 2013:

> Myron went mountain biking with me this morning. We took a customer with us. It was a pretty easy trail, but Justin, the customer, was not in good shape, so it took us forever to go a couple of miles. However, Myron has become a pretty good mountain biker.
>
> I am trying to get "likes" on my Facebook page for the South Pole Epic. Hopefully, a good presence on Facebook will help when we go after sponsors. Danae has been helping me to try and get more likes. It is cool that she is trying to help.

So it was that Daniel dealt with where he was going and what he was going there to do.

---

[10] Postmortem note: "It turned out that I failed to get the fundraising to work." In the end, he just went ahead and hocked his life. He took out a second mortgage. He risked everything to get out on the ice and then he risked everything to get across the ice to his goal at the Pole. Daniel's final judgment was that "… nothing could be as difficult as the trip itself." Wayne Gretzky said, "You miss 100% of the shots you don't take."

What is Antarctica?

First of all, there is no place on earth like Antarctica. Not even the Arctic Ocean is as remote from human society or from anything associated with the climate of Planet Earth. As Daniel dug in to the information, he learned that Antarctica is a desert. Just as the desert is blowing grains of sand, so Antarctica is blowing grains of ice. As in any other desert, Sahara or Antarctica, humidity is extremely low and there is very little precipitation.

The solid, ancient ice that covers the continent makes a dome that is 9,301 feet above sea level at the South Pole, but the rock of the continental land is only 300 feet above sea level at the South Pole, so the ice there is 9,000 feet thick. And the South Pole is not the highest point on the continent nor is it in the center of the continent. Daniel stood in front of his bicycle shop and looked out over Utah Valley with Utah Lake covering its floor and imagined the valley filled with ice to a height 2,000 feet above the crest of Mount Timpanogos.

Antarctica is losing mass, polar orbit satellites reveal, because—just like a huge glacier—the ice is flowing down the rock slope of the shallow, upside down saucer that is the continental dome. Glaciers teach us that water is a fluid even when it is an extremely slow flowing frozen fluid.

The same rock carving action of glacier flow causes a "pebbling" of the Antarctic ice dome. These endless little hills, kind of like a landscape of giant bumps or moguls, are one hundred to two hundred feet from crest to trough and fill the Antarctic plain the whole way from coast to polar plateau, 700 miles, dropping 9000 feet from center of continental mass to coast. Super cold air in the center of the continent flows over these thousands of hills or bumps down the slope towards the coast. The winds do not swirl or gust but are rather a constant strong headwind for the traveler from coast to pole. These are the *katabatic* winds of the Antarctic high desert.

Ambush of the killer katabatics.

Note: *Wikipedia* says that katabatic winds are so called because the Greek word *katabatikos* means "flowing downhill." Thus, winds that flow down mountain sides fluted or grooved into a succession of fingers and draws are pulled downhill deep into the draws both by gravity and by the power of the cold air inversion. Daniel knew all about the "canyon winds" of Utah and the "Santa Ana" winds out of California. These Antarctic katabatic winds flowed down the inverted saucer of the polar ice cap. So when Daniel struggled up the ice cap toward the Pole, the katabatic winds fell upon him, blasting him in the face and on the hands that gripped the handlebars.

Katabatic winds make sastrugi. On top of *Wikipedia*, we have Daniel Burton's definition: "Sastrugi are created by the actions of the wind and sun on the snow in polar regions. First the wind blows the snow, creating snow drifts. The sun hits different parts of the drifted snow at different angles. As the sun hits the snow it transforms it into ice, but the ice is harder where the angle of the sun is more direct. The katabatic winds of Antarctica return and carve away the soft snow leaving behind the hardest ice. It is really Mother Nature's method of doing ice sculptures. These ice sculptures frequently have sharp two to three foot drops, but they can get to be as big as 10 foot drops," down which, of course, Daniel (and any other expeditionary who left behind all roads and went cross country) had to roll on his bicycle. Daniel would later modestly report that he went around the ten foot drops. He only swooped down the two to four foot sheer drops.

All the explorers agreed, Antarctica seems to be another planet, another world, with its own laws of climatology. Like all of the great deserts of Planet Earth, there is no forgiveness of error in Antarctica. Daniel learned the soft snow would be one of his worst enemies. A nice firm base under the snow made biking still possible, but the sleds would be a lot harder to pull and the traction would be low requiring a very low tire pressure.

Daniel would have to bike over thousands of narrow slit crevasses that were like cracks in an asphalt road—only these cracks could be a thousand feet deep, if only five inches wide. There were also the big crevasses—as in our popular, movie fed imagination—that could not be "jumped" even with a good run on a fat wheeled bicycle. ALE used ground penetrating radar to identify the larger crevasses and plan a route for Daniel that went around those, making the route longer and using up more of the finite time he had.

Daniel the computer guy then did research on contemporary Antarctic explorers. These were the ones he would learn from and compete with.

42

Douglas Stoup created a guide-exploration-charity fundraising company called "Ice Ax Expeditions." Doug's company had many adventures in both the Arctic and the Antarctic and everyplace in between. Doug led expeditions that simply walked to the North Pole or to the South Pole. His expeditions studied Arctic ice melt and Antarctic routes to the pole never used before. Doug stoup was an early experimenter with bicycles operating on snow and ice. In 2003, he developed what he called an "ice bike" with super wide tires but small diameter wheels. He tried out his ice bike on a 200 mile bike expedition in Antarctica that went around the Heritage mountain range. He didn't go from coast to pole, but his expedition did prove the concept Daniel was looking for.

Daniel had bought a Stoup style "fat bike" in the winter of 2012 and ridden across frozen Utah Lake. Out on that frozen surface, the seed was planted, a seed that had grown into a bike expedition to the South Pole. Some people have ideas, others execute them. Burton has always been an executor of ideas, whether it was through inventing and patenting software, opening a bicycle shop, or embarking on a life-changing ride across the most formidable landscape in the world. Daniel describes this formative time for his ideas. "I had people ask me about fat bikes in the fall and winter of 2012, so, in December, I decided to buy four fat bikes to use as rental bikes. We used the bikes to ride across Utah Lake and I did a lot of biking on the snow covered trails of the nearby mountains."

Aaron Linsdau set the record for the most days to get to the South Pole. He took 81 days to get to the Pole. When most people would have given up, he continued on. Daniel wrote in his research notes, "I felt I needed to train myself mentally to be prepared to continue on no matter what. This is as important, or maybe more important than any physical training I can do. I want to have the perseverance of Aaron. I have to draw on that mental toughness preparation in order to finish."

Helen Skelton is a BBC broadcast journalist and extreme athlete who has hosted or been a guest on numerous British and world educational and charitable fundraising BBC television programs. Her intersection with Daniel Burton is her exploration of the limits of human capability. She hosted *Blue Peter*, a BBC children's science show. She kayaked the length of the Amazon to raise awareness of the plight of the Amazon Basin and its indigenous peoples. She was the "gutsy bird" who did a six mile run with the British Royal Marines. Also, she was not hard to look at on the red carpet before her big charity events.

In January, 2012, before Daniel Burton had even begun to formulate his plan, Helen Skelton carried out hers.

Muscleprodigy.com reported:

> She snow kited 329 miles, snow shoed 68 miles and biked 103 miles to complete her 500-mile journey in just 18 days. The average temperature during this time of year in that area is between -15 and -50 degrees Celsius. Not to mention, she had to endure hurricane-like [katabatic] winds, huge cliffs of ice [sastrugi] and super deep snow [super deep snow. It's a technical term].

Helen is the first to do a multi-sport, kite, ski, and bike expedition to the South Pole. Juan Menéndez Granados followed in her footsteps, skiing and biking to the South Pole. Skelton choose to use a special bike, in which the tires of the bike are flat and tubeless to avoid being ripped up by the ice. The tires were 20 inches high so that she could ride through the deep snow. The bike weighed a total of 40 pounds, just 10 pounds more than the average mountain bike. Her bike was the same as designed by Doug Stoup and was nearly identical to the one he used in his historic first Antarctica bike expedition.

Muscle Prodigy's account went on.

> She had such bad blisters that they required at least 15 meters of medical tape. She said there would be a different pain every day from the cycling, skiing, and kite skiing. She also added that when you kite ski there was burning on the face from the wind and your hands freeze as well.

Daniel would blog and journal about that a lot.

> To pass the time during the journey, she would play games in her head, such as going through the alphabet and trying to name as many countries for each letter as she could

Daniel would pass the time with observations on spirituality, existentialism, and how hungry and tired he was.

> "Skelton has done many impressive feats before so she is not new to this kind of stuff. She previously high-wire walked between [two] chimneys of Battersea power station in London."

And in Antarctica she would ski?… kite?… bike? That requires some explanation. She did all three on her expedition. At times she used a kite to pull her. This is a popular form of travel in Antarctica. Other times she skied like most other expeditions do. She also rode the bike at times. This beautiful adventuress was also showcased in all of these activities by a full film crew driving along with her on the ice (or, in the case of the Amazon, power boating down the river in front of her)

Her critics were harsh, but Daniel well understood that Helen Skelton biked, skied, and kited for the purpose of showcasing on television the ways that people could deal with the Antarctic or any extreme environment. When she hitched herself to a kite, she was swept along by the katabatic winds working in her favor, pulling her down the road. It was Helen's Antarctic analogue of wind surfing.

Helen was and is a celebrity who uses interest in her goings on to dramatize great causes. Whatever she or her press secretary might say about the Amazon or the high wire act, her Antarctic expedition was the first to arrive at the pole on a bike, but was not considered a bike expedition by the adventure community. Helen Skelton of the BBC had the journalistic integrity to never claim otherwise. For Daniel Burton, as the Mormon missionaries say, the "field is all white and ready to harvest." (St. John 4:35) The stage was set for a coast to pole bike expedition.

Maria Leijerstam is described by the press as a "British adventurer." A 35 year old Welsh woman, daughter of Adrienne Leijerstam, this ultramarathon runner trained in the Welsh Vale (Valley) of Clamorgan to be the first to *tricycle* from the Antarctic coast at the top of McMurdo Sound, the deepest indentation into the Antarctic continent. She would be in Daniel's cohort, starting on December 7, 2013, and tricycling along the "South Pole Highway." As *Wikipedia* notes, the South Pole Highway is a compacted ice roadway (for Antarctica, an "improved road") maintained and marked with flags by the U.S. Government to carry supplies to South Pole Station. Any crevasses it crosses have been dynamited and filled in.

She traveled a little more than 300 miles using a recumbent trike designed and built by Ice Trikes, Ltd. Determined to beat all the expeditions coming in January of 2014 (which included Daniel's South Pole Epic), Maria got to the Pole in ten days, fourteen hours.

She had no kite and no skis. It was the first cycling only trip to the South Pole. It was a great ride and set the record as the first recumbent trike ride from coast to Pole, albeit from a deep indentation that, compared to the other cycling expeditions, halved the distance to the Pole.

She had intended to do it as a real expedition carrying all her gear, but the trike could not handle it, so to insure she would arrive at the South Pole first she abandoned the expedition aspects and focused on the documentary aspects (See *White Ice Cycle* on ITV). Daniel was told that to keep warm when she stopped to rest, she would join her gear in the truck to take breaks from the wind and cold. Maria told the world she couldn't have done it without her mummy…her journalist PR consultant mother, Adrienne Leijerstam, who manages and promotes all her expeditions and events.

Her bicycle was actually a tricycle. Daniel points out, "A bicyclist cannot slow down past the point of losing balance and falling over. A tricyclist can slow to a literal human crawl. That meant Maria could slow down enough to keep from getting sweat soaked and risking freezing to death, an option not available to someone on a bike."

Eric Larsen…There can be only one.

Eric was the only explorer-adventurer and extreme athlete besides Daniel Burton who was truly in the hunt for the title of first bicycle expedition from the perimeter coast to the Pole without compromising expedition parameters in order to get there. Eric Larsen also used a fat bike on his expedition to the South Pole. Eric traveled one fourth of the distance from coast to pole. At the time, it was enough to set a record for the most progress made towards the pole by bike and for the longest bike ride in Antarctica. Daniel remembers, "I followed his expedition until he turned around." What happened?

Daniel Burton came to adventure, exploration, and advocacy from a career as a computer programmer. Eric Larsen was a career explorer and expeditionary guide. Eric was determined to do it right…fat tired bicycle, all gear and supplies in pannier bags, no skis, kites, or trucks, no prepared roadway, pedaling over the crevasses alone and unsupported (except for food dropped at GPS recorded waypoints along the route that he had to find if he wanted to eat and, in that cold, it was eat a lot or die quick). He started out from Hercules Inlet on the Antarctic coast straight south from Cape Horn at the bottom of South America, from near sea level at the coast, with a goal of reaching the pole at 9,301 feet.

All private Antarctic expeditions are monitored and supported by ALE. If you want to try your luck (or God's patience) with an expedition to the South Pole, you have to pay ALE a fee for all the way in *and all the way out*. Eric was an "all in" kind of extreme explorer adventurer. If Eric completed a round trip by bike, he would be refunded the cost of the unused airplane return trip. That was a nice feature of the ALE contract, but it turned out to be an enemy of mental toughness. The refund weighed heavily on Eric's mind and factored into his turning around, making his expedition a round trip rather than a more expensive oneway trip. It was the out you don't need when you have committed to a deed that is nearly impossible.

Just for comparison, Daniel Burton paid for one way only, coast to pole and fly out. Daniel would have no refund for completing a round trip. He had no motivation to return to the starting location. Indeed, he had to make sure he didn't get to the Pole too late for the last flight out.

Eric Larsen had paid his fee and paid his dues. He was prepared and positioned to set out, but Eric Larsen had trouble in mind. All the great athletes — and explorer adventurers — say that, at the highest level, the hardest part of the game or the feat is not the physical part, but the mental toughness. When Eric set off from Hercules Inlet on his fat tired snow bike on December 20, 2012, he was concerned about the family he had left back in Colorado. The next day he wrote in his blog, "I didn't want to get up this morning. What was I thinking coming to Antarctica to try this thing — biking to the South Pole? 'A crazy idea,' I said to myself out loud."

And the day after that he wrote, "I am rooted in the here and now staring across one of the most remote and inhospitable places in the entire world and a goal I'm not sure I'll be able to achieve." He got a quarter of the way to the Pole and then he turned his bike around and went back to Hercules Inlet, claiming his refund of his return trip fee. Family first. It wasn't his time. It wasn't his turn.

Let it be said that Eric Larsen's "Cycle South" expedition in 2012 may not have succeeded in getting to the South Pole, but it did succeed in proving that the bike could be used for a South Pole expedition. His March 2014 expedition, "Last North," on the other hand, was an inspiring success. To dramatize the apparently irreversible melting of the polar ice cap over the Arctic Ocean, Eric Larsen and Ryan Waters set out from Canada's Ellesmere Island to ski, snowshoe, and even swim over the shifting ice floes and in the melting slush of the Arctic Ocean all the way to the North Pole, 630 miles away. No trucks allowed.

Daniel Burton considered the effort of Eric Larsen and concluded that he could and should use Eric's concept. It was the right way to accomplish the mission. It seemed that Eric could have made it to the Pole but most likely could not have ridden his bike back to the start. We may never know the full reasons why he turned around, but it inspired Daniel to not allow external influences or self doubt to turn him back. Daniel said, "I recalculated what I had to do to not quit. I could only pay what I could handle. I could do this with the money I had and that left me with no choice but to get to the Pole in time for my prepaid flight. My family was OK in a way that his was not. I wouldn't have tried if Eric had not tried. What he experienced taught me how to not have a breaking point." Daniel convinced his mind that it was impossible to quit.

Daniel met Eric at the Outdoor Retailers' Convention in the summer of 2013. Daniel studied Eric for principles, concepts, and techniques that would make his own expedition a success. Somehow, the spirit of that conversation got confused by misunderstanding and darkened by hurt feelings. "In an interview Eric gave later to an outdoor wilderness website," Daniel mourns, "Eric said that I said I was happy he had failed because now I could accomplish the feat he had tried for." Daniel says, "Actually, what I meant to get across was that I was grateful that Eric had laid the foundation. He showed that biking to the South Pole was possible." Daniel thinks he lost the opportunity to acknowledge a friendship with the man whose career taught him what he needed to know to succeed.

Why Didn't He Make It?

Daniel wondered about Eric's expedition. To ride successfully, Daniel had to plan successfully. That meant he had to answer that question. Eric Larsen was the most thoughtful, the most prepared, the most experienced explorer of extreme environments with a bicycle. His expeditions had powerful purpose and aided human progress in environmentalism and personal development. Daniel wrote, "But, it gets me thinking. Why didn't Eric make it? I read his blog. He had a little kid that he didn't want to be away from for that long. He talks about how he might not be able to complete the trip in most posts. Did he just not really want to do it? It is an incredible feat so I feel bad even doubting his resolve. Why then didn't his expedition succeed? His bike weighed 130+ pounds. He was pushing it uphill and through soft snow. The winds were strong and I assume the panniers caught a lot of wind. Maybe he could have made it if he wasn't doing it solo and carrying his own gear... ten days and he went 175 miles, actually less than 10 days because day 10 was headed back, and the first day or two were getting to the start. So he had to have averaged more than 17.5 miles per day. I read about Hannah McKeand's record breaking trip to the South Pole. Eric averaged more miles per day than Hannah did. Why did he not make it? Then I looked at the time table. Hannah started in mid-November; Eric started in late December. The trip needed to be completed by January 20 when the camps at the Pole and Union Glacier closed. So, while Eric's number of days to complete was possible, his late start made it so he would be at the South Pole after the drop dead date."

Back in the non-Antarctic world, Daniel analyzed his conversation with Eric about everything that had happened. Daniel thought he knew what had been Eric's dilemma. He realized that Eric's situation was really very simple, if heartbreaking. Eric had to go home and take care of his family. It was just that simple. Later, when Daniel performed the analysis of Eric's expedition that was necessary for his own planning, he realized that Eric went to Antarctica and, back home in Colorado, something came up. It just happened. Daniel says, "When I talked to him about the expedition he said it was just the wrong time in his life." How grateful Daniel became that his own family didn't run into trouble while he was on his epic ride.

"Juan Sin Miedo" ("Juan Without Fear" aka "Fearless John") Juan Menéndez Granados of Spain has always promulgated his own self-styled title as Europe's greatest extreme explorer mountain biker. He wanted to take his skill and his knowledge and achieve some great advancement in his sport. Daniel Burton and Juan Menéndez hit upon the same idea—to bicycle to the South Pole from the edge of the Antarctic continent. They would rely on the same equipment, the fat tired snow bike. They had the same idea but different execution plans. Juan Menéndez would pull his sled with his bike when he could and pull his bike *in* his sled on skis when he could not ride. Daniel would not have any skis. He would make it or not—maybe quite literally live or die—on his bike or his feet. There was another difference that Daniel would not call a relevant alibi. Daniel turned 50 while on the expedition. Juan Menéndez was out there on the ice at about half Daniel's age.

Natalio Cosoy writing for the BBC European News called it this way:

An Antarctic bike ride to the South Pole

Since Roald Amundsen's Norwegian expedition first conquered the South Pole in 1911 plenty of others have followed in his footsteps - but not necessarily by foot.

The journey has been completed with dog sleds, snowmobiles and four-wheel-drives. But no one had ever completed it on a pushbike. That is the challenge Juan Menéndez Granados has set for himself. And he plans to do it solo. . . .

"I have been preparing for this challenge for two and a half years," he tells BBC Mundo.

That training has included an expedition in its own right—a 27-day cycle-ride through Greenland in August-September this year.

While in the dining tent at the base camp, Juan Menéndez confessed to Daniel and others at the table that his trip across Greenland had not really been a bike ride. He said that he had found the conditions unsuitable for a bike and really it had been much more of a ski expedition than a bike expedition. Then he told the people at the table that he would not claim to do something that he really didn't do. This was a promise that he later would not keep when it came to his claim to have biked across Antarctica.

Natalio of the BBC went on to say,

Being alone will bring its own complications. Loneliness will have an emotional impact. But it also means he will have no assistance on hand if he needs to be rescued.

In good weather conditions a rescue party would take five hours to reach him, according to Stephen Jones, member of the Royal Geographical Society and manager of Antarctic Logistics and Expeditions (ALE), which will support Menéndez Granados.

"Worst case scenario," says Jones, "he might have to wait a few days for good weather."

In bad weather a rescue operation could take days to reach him.

The bike. Jones agrees it is a very difficult enterprise. "He's got a greater risk of mechanical failure [than someone skiing or walking]."

But the latest evolution in bicycle design has been key in allowing adventurers to try their luck in Antarctica - Menéndez Granados's bike has 12cm (4.7 in) wheels and modified forks. He has decided against using tyres with nails but says the broader tyres should provide the grip he needs.

Stephen Jones, Manager Antarctic Logistics and Expeditions (ALE): "Several people have tried it over a few years, and none of them got anywhere at all, until last year," says Jones.

Then Natalio got to Daniel's expedition.

He will not be the only one. The American Daniel Burton will also try to reach the South Pole on a solo trip on two wheels, and is leaving around the same time. And by the end of 2014 the Australian Kate Leeming will attempt the challenge." [At that time, Natalio didn't know what Daniel was finding out, that Kate couldn't do it this year]

Going on, Natalio wrote,

It looks like a race then. But the Spaniard disagrees: "Antarctica is not a good place for races."

Juan Menéndez would publicly claim that it was not a race, and when talking with Daniel would feign that it was not a race, but his every action indicated that to him it was a race, that no matter what, he had to arrive at the South Pole before Daniel.

Although it is considered a cycling expedition, there will be times when he will have to dismount, put the bike on the sled and pull.

Quoting Juan Menéndez: "I will try to do as much as possible on the bicycle and in normal conditions it should be considered a bike expedition."

Juan Menéndez was unable to fulfill this goal. When he would call in to ALE, he would say that he just didn't find the conditions suitable to biking. In his blog, he stated that he did not even use his bike for the first 10 days. It was true that the biking those first 10 days was extremely difficult, but as Daniel proved, there were small sections that were very rideable and large sections that were possible but extremely difficult. However, if one is wearing skis it is hard to pedal a bike. The time required to take off skis, get a bike out of the sled and put the skis into the sled, and then the time to go from bike back to skis would have consumed a great deal of travel time. In other words, using skis prevented one from doing what could honestly be considered a bicycle expedition.

Natalio went back to his interview of Jones from ALE.

"There are bits where you have to walk," says Jones, who adds that Menéndez Granados will be carrying skis to use when pedaling becomes impossible, especially on soft snow where walking would also be hard.

But if he skis in certain stretches, would he then be able to claim he was the first person to reach the South Pole by bike? . . .

Jones believes that it could be claimed that he did it by bike if he spends some 30 days pedaling and the rest on skis.

From the tracks left behind by Menéndez, Daniel calculated that, in the end, Juan Menéndez had skied approximately 85% of the time and rode his bike fewer than 120 of the 750 miles, not even coming close to the 30 days of biking that Jones would need to be able to count this as a biking expedition.

An honorable and elegant exchange: Daniel had a long, thoughtful, email exchange with Kate Leeming, the Australian cyclist who had contemplated a South Polar expedition. The conversation became a reaching out between Daniel and Juan Menéndez.

Daniel had emailed Kate Leeming of Australia and Juan Menéndez of Spain about the three of them going on expedition together. He wrote:

> Kate and Juan Menéndez:
>
> I have finally gotten the funds to do my South Pole expedition. Now that I know for sure I will be able to go on my expedition I was wondering if you would be willing to talk about different aspects of our expeditions.
>
> I know that we are all competing to be the first to bike to the South Pole, but I have decided to base my plans on what gives me the best odds of completing a round trip journey, and not really worry about if one of you beats me to the pole."

Later on, Dan would really worry, as we shall see.

> Anyway, given that we are all working towards the same thing I thought it might be nice to start a conversation with each other.
>
> Thanks
> Daniel Burton

Kate replied back that she was glad to hear that Daniel was able to do the expedition but that she would need to postpone her expedition, hopefully being able to go in the 2014/2015 season. She was engaged in many good causes around the world and this Antarctic extreme expedition could not be her top priority at this time. She wished Daniel all the best, but "being first" was only of value if it attracted attention to a cause.

Daniel responded.

Daniel to Kate and Juan Menéndez:

I feel the same, being first is a good marketing point for getting sponsorship, but mostly it is the privilege of cycling to the South Pole. I wish you the best of luck and for sure will follow your progress when you set out on your expedition.

I just found the Explorer Web story about Juan's trip across Greenland. Good job Juan!

Thanks

Daniel Burton

Juan Menéndez replied back congratulating Daniel and Kate on their efforts, and indicated that he did not have the money for the expedition yet. He was trying to keep the costs down to the minimum. This would mean that he would have to do the expedition with no resupplies and would only be able to attempt a one way expedition.

Kate replied back talking about the difficulties of finding a sponsorship and asking about Juan's Greenland trip. She was hoping to be able to do that trip the following spring.

Juan Menéndez then sent an email to Daniel asking for details about his expedition. It was apparent that Juan Menéndez was realizing that Daniel's expedition would be competing with Juan's as the first real bike expedition to the South Pole.

Daniel probably should have kept his plans to himself instead of helping his competition by revealing details about his plan, but Daniel tended to be an open and honest man and didn't hold anything back.

Daniel replied back:

When I first started seriously thinking about doing this expedition I talked to a friend, Todd, about having him go with me. He really wanted to do it with as much support as he could get. Just being able to bike to the South Pole was my real desire, so I was willing to do it with snowmobiles, but in my heart I liked the idea of doing it without snowmobiles. However, getting funding, as you know, is extremely difficult.

53

I was only able to get enough money for one person to go to the South Pole. I really would like to do the trip back to the start but I don't have enough funds for a round trip. I will have three resupplies... I think it gives me a much greater chance of succeeding.

I'm excited about the Borealis bike, but also a bit scared. I still do not have the bike. It is supposed to get here in a couple of weeks, and then I have to put it together. I am worried about using a new bike that has not been tested at -40°. I'm also just nervous about not having spent time riding that bike. However, I think the light weight and the ability to have racks mounted to the bike will make this a great bike for the expedition.

I read Eric Larsen's log of his attempt to bike to the South Pole. It seemed to me that his heavy bike and the wind resistance of the panniers were a big part of his problems. I was thinking that having the gear in a pulk would be more aerodynamic and would help the tires stay on top of the snow.

Okay, time out! What is a pulk? Wikipedia says: "A pulk (from Finnish pulkka) is a Nordic, short, low-slung, small toboggan used in sport or for transport, pulled by a dog or a skier or in Lapland, pulled by reindeer. The sled can be used to carry supplies such as a tent or food, or transport a child or other person. In Norway, pulks are often used by families with small children on skiing trips (small children being pulled by the parents). In Sweden, pulks are often used, mostly by children, as a winter toy for going downhill. Pulks are nowadays made of plastic, which makes them cheap to buy. A larger pulk, designed for transporting larger amounts of goods, is called *ahkio* in Finnish. This word is also used by the US Army for a human-drawn snow sled."

Daniel to Juan Menéndez continuing:

So my plan was to pull the gear on a pulk. A guy in England gave me some pulks. I then talked to Eric Larsen and he thought that pulks were a bad idea because ice on the plateau is rough and hard to pull a pulk on. So I decided to use a combination of pulk and panniers. I can move the gear all onto the pulk if that is what is working best, or I can move most of the gear into the panniers if needed. Talking with ALE they think this is a good plan and like the idea of adjusting the load based on the changing conditions.

Eric had been to the South Pole on skis so he was familiar with the conditions there. Indeed, the last 20 miles before the pole greeted Daniel with soft snow that was very difficult to pull a sled through; however, after experimenting with both sled and panniers in the soft snow near the coast, Daniel had learned that even when the sleds were hard to pull they were better than putting the weight on the bike causing the wheels to sink into the snow.

Daniel blogged:

I am scheduled to fly to Union Glacier on 23 November. There are a couple of ski expeditions that are going on that same flight. I will spend a little time at Union Glacier to make sure everything is good. This means that the ski expeditions will start before me. If their tracks don't get covered by snow I will follow them past the crevasse fields.

ALE showed me Eric's mileage log. He traveled about 20 miles per day. At that rate it would take 35 days. I'm probably a little over confident right now. I think it would be cool to do the expedition in less than 24 days and if things work out that is what I will try and do. However, my number one goal is to get to the South Pole, so I have everything in place to have it be a 50 day trip and will make getting there a priority over getting there fast.

A *little* over confident? How about a *lot* over confident. It would take Daniel more than twice as long as he was hoping. However, he planned well and made sure he was prepared for the worst.

Daniel's email to Juan and Kate continues:

I'm jealous of your expedition across Greenland. I wish I had the chance to get great training like that. Both you and Kate have great expedition experience that I am lacking.

Getting the money is so hard. I thought this was such an amazing expedition that sponsors would like the publicity and I would be able to get funding. But it just didn't happen that way. Not too long ago I was at the point that time had run out, and I didn't have the money. It was really hard to think that I wouldn't be able to go this year. Fortunately I was able to get a loan to pay for the expedition. I am taking a big financial risk doing this expedition, but it is just something I can't bear not doing. I wish you the best of luck. I know how it feels to be focusing so hard on getting the expedition funded. I really hope you are able to get the funds you need.

Thanks

Daniel Burton

Juan Menéndez again emailed Daniel and Kate and told them that he had not been able to ride his bike in Greenland, even without carrying his own gear, and that Greenland was no good for cycling. Antarctica, he assumed, would be more predictable and more suitable to biking. This email was a harbinger of how his expedition to the South Pole would also turn into a ski expedition rather than a bike expedition.

Daniel Burton sends — 12 October 2013:

Good luck. Hope to see you there. I know I am struggling to get everything ready in time. A lot to do and so little time left. Headed South?

I just saw this story. http://www.bbc.co.uk/news/world-europe-24728869

Does that mean you are going to be there? It would be great to see you down there. I was starting to worry you wouldn't make it because the crowd funding doesn't look like it is going to get the money you need.

Hope to see you soon.

Daniel Burton

All My Bags Are Packed

I'm ready to go. The preparations for the expedition were progressing and it was time to start packing. Daniel explained some of those final preparations.

"I secured a sponsorship with DHL where they would ship my bike and gear to Antarctica and then back home after the expedition. The ReadyStore agreed to sponsor me by providing all the food I would need for the expedition. Borealis Bikes, Shimano, e*thirteen, Xpedo, and Giant contributed the parts to build up my bike. All of the parts for the bike arrived just in time for me to build the bike, take it for a couple of test rides and then pack it into a large wooden crate. When building the bike, I disassembled shifters and bearings, replacing the factory supplied grease with grease designed for -40° F temperatures. I then took shrink tubing designed for electrical wires and shrink wrapped my brake and derailleur cables to strengthen them for the extreme cold.

"I needed to anticipate what things could go wrong with the bike and how I could fix the problems in order to continue with the expedition. I was worried about the carbon fiber bike frame. Would it hold up in -40° F temperatures? It was a brand new company with a brand new bike, so it had never been tested in the extreme cold. What if it broke? Then I learned about a new product called FiberFix. It was like the material doctors use to create a cast for broken bones. FiberFix could be used to repair a break in the frame or in a tent pole or in who knows what else. It was a new product that had received a lot of publicity, so it was hard to find, but eventually I found some in a hardware store. A good farmer can fix just about anything with duct tape and bailing wire, so I took a roll of duct tape with me. Also, the FiberFix would work as the ultimate duct tape for extreme repairs. After getting the FiberFix and duct tape, I asked for some bailing wire. I found some tie wire that was a thinner gauge than the bailing wire. My Canada Goose parka had a wire in the hood that made it so you could shape the hood around your face. I took some tie wire for emergency repairs, and then I took some more and put it in the seam of the hood on my light Columbia jacket.

"With the bike all prepared for the expedition, I now needed to figure out what extra parts to bring. I would be pulling a lot of weight in the sleds. I got two 18" pieces of galvanized pipe and drilled holes in each end of the pipe. On the one end of each pipe I bolted a mount used for pulling bike trailers, and I put an eye hook on the other end. I could then mount a pipe on each side of the rear hub, and use a carabiner to hook a rope to the bike. I was worried that pulling over 150 pounds of gear could break the skewer, so an extra skewer made the list of items. The chain drive is essential to being able to bike. It is possible to remove links, shortening the chain for an emergency repair, but I figured the consequences of losing a chain were too great, so a spare chain made the list.

"On my mountain bike, I have switched to tubeless tires, and I frequently go mountain biking without a spare tube. There have been a few times I have gotten a flat and had to walk back to the road, but it was infrequent enough that I would take the risk. I built my training bike with a tubeless setup, but I was worried that the sealant used in the tires could freeze in Antarctica so I decided to stick with tubes for my expedition bike. Now how many spare tubes should I take? There will be no thorns, nails, or other items that could give me a flat. The biggest risk I could think of was a pinch flat from low pressure, or the tube just cracking because it was so cold. I decided to take two extra tubes, and two hand pumps. I would need to be able to adjust air pressure based on riding conditions, so a pump was critical. But will the plastic or the o-rings in the pump endure the cold? I took two pumps just in case.

"One of the major problems with biking in extreme conditions can be the freehub, the ratcheting part in the rear hub that propels the bike when pedaling and spins when coasting. The freehub has small spring loaded pawls that could get frozen, making it so pedaling would not propel the bike. On the back shelf of my bike shop I had an extra freehub. I considered taking it with me, but I had to decide which extra parts to take and which to leave behind. Taking a full backup bike was just not practical. The rear hub was really easy to disassemble, giving me access to the small parts of the freehub. I figured this would allow me to fix a frozen freehub. If I had a catastrophic failure of the freehub I could use the tie wire to wire the gears to the spokes and keep going. Given that I could easily maintain the freehub and I had a backup plan, the extra freehub did not make the list of essential items.

"My family room was turned into a staging area for the expedition. Media didn't appreciate the mess of tent, sleeping bag, air mattress, solar panels, cameras, camp equipment and other expedition items laid out all over the floor, but in spite of the annoying mess she agreed to do some sewing projects. I needed bags for my sleds, so we took some denim fabric that had been in Media's supply of fabric for a dozen years, and made two custom duffle bag style bags with zippers running the length of each bag. Then came a bigger challenge for my wife—sewing the fur ruff onto my lighter weight jacket. I needed a light jacket for biking that would protect me from the wind but is breathable to keep me dry. I picked out a Columbia jacket, which, of course, does not have a fur lined hood. Whenever I stopped the first thing I did was pull out the Canada Goose parka and put it on. The last thing I would do before starting to ride was take the parka off and put it into the sleds.

"My wife hates germs and so touching animal fur was an almost unbearable thought, but I needed a fur ruff on my jacket. With a lot of nagging, I finally convinced her to sew a zipper onto a fur ruff and onto my jacket. I was very happy with my light jacket that was now converted into an Antarctica expedition jacket. One more sewing job: I got some Smith goggles. I needed to sew a mask onto the bottom of the goggles. I needed to be sure that there would be no gaps between the goggles and the mask. Any gaps and the cold katabatic winds would give me frostbite in minutes or even seconds. I bought several neoprene ski masks and my wife cut them apart and sewed them together to make two masks that were then sewn onto the bottoms of the goggles."

Journal—2 November 2013:

Less than two weeks until I fly down to Chile to begin my expedition to the South Pole. I still have a lot to do. I haven't tested any of my methods of pulling a sled. I haven't done anything like this before. I really am taking on a lot with little experience, yet I somehow feel this is going to work out just fine. I sent my crate with bike, food, and gear down to Chile. I'm worried about the contents all getting there in good condition. Also I know I need to make sure I have everything I need either in that box or with me when I leave home. Once I get to Antarctica I can't say, 'Oops, I forgot something,' and then get it from someone or somewhere. I can't have any game ending omissions.

On November 9th, with time running out, Juan Menéndez emailed Daniel saying he still did not have the money and was working hard to get the bank to lend him the money.

Daniel started to consider the possibility of working together. Maybe by allowing Juan Menéndez to share the food in Daniel's caches he could help Juan Menéndez lighten his load without increasing his cost for the expedition. In exchange, Daniel hoped that two people working together would have better odds of success than two people working independently. He wrote:

Juan,

Would you be interested in working together on our expeditions? I know your plan is for a solo unassisted, unsupported expedition.

If you would be interested in working together maybe we could share my three resupply caches, and as we travel over softer snow we could take turns breaking trail. If you are interested let me know and we can see if we can work something out. If you're not interested that is fine also.

Thanks,

Dan

Daniel didn't understand Juan's reply when Juan said he wanted to be "collaborative" but wanted to stay solo. Was this intended to be misleading?

Daniel wrote,

To Juan:

I fly down to Punta Arenas this Friday, and then to Union Glacier on the 23rd. My bike and gear are in Santiago today. They have to go the rest of the way by truck because the crate is too big to go by plane. I wanted them to be in Punta Arenas before I left Utah, but it looks like they won't get there until after I get there.

Let me know how things are going for you.

Wish you the best of luck,

Dan

Juan Menéndez wrote back a vague message, but it seemed that he was finding a way to get to Antarctica. Juan Menéndez wrote, "I'm looking forward to meeting you."

Daniel wrote back—13 November 2013:

Juan,

See you soon. It is crazy for me to be able to get everything done in time. It has to be even more crazy for you.

Daniel Burton

Daniel wrote to Juan Menéndez again.

So, are you able to get your bike to go by plane all the way to Punta Arenas? I was told the max size is 3 feet and since my frame is longer than 3 feet that it would not be able to fly. I'm in a bit of a panic right now because my bike and gear are stuck in Santiago trying to get through customs. ALE says that customs is on strike and the borders are closed. It takes 5 days to get the shipment from Santiago to Punta Arenas, so I don't know if it will get there in time.

Juan Menéndez replied that he was going to be flying with all his gear and his bike, but that he still didn't have his bike.

"Wow, and I thought I was late getting my bike," Daniel recounts.

Daniel's expedition crate was supposed to fly from Salt Lake City, Utah to Santiago, Chile. Because the crate was too big for the planes that fly between Santiago and Punta Arenas, it would then have to proceed by truck through Argentina and then back into Chile. The crate was addressed to Antarctica, which should have allowed it to pass through Chile and Argentina without having to pay for customs. However, there was a problem with the way it was transferred from air freight to ground freight, which this meant it had to clear customs in Chile and incurred significant customs import fees, as well as delayed its arrival in Punta Arenas.

With the crate on its way south, it was now time for Daniel to start going south.

Blog — 15 November 2013:

I'm leaving on a jet plane

All my bags are packed. I'm ready to go...

(Well, mostly the song doesn't fit but skipping to the chorus...)

Cause I'm leavin' on a jet plane

Don't know when I'll be back again

Oh babe, I can't wait to go [Yes, this is Daniel's ironic parody. He knew very well that it was "Oh, Babe, I hate to go.]

My bike and gear are on an adventure of their own. Hoping they are in Punta Arenas soon!

Sandy Point (Punta Arenas). After nearly a year of preparation, Burton boarded an airplane and set out for Punta Arenas, Chile. Despite plenty of dissuasion, Burton was executing his idea. While his biggest fans, family and friends thought his idea was "cool," even his most ardent supporters now tell him, "We thought you were going to die out there." But he didn't die. He blogged to the world and journaled to himself.

The story inside…Journal — 15 November 2013:

The journey begins. I am at the airport waiting for my first flight. My bags are heavy. I have two suitcases. Together they were over 80 pounds. I also have a carry-on that feels very heavy. Then, add all the stuff I have in the crate. I think my weight is too much. I may have to lose some things to keep the weight down. A lot of my weight is electronics. I want to have what I need to make a great record of the expedition. Upon completion, more data will help tell a better story and I need to be able to sell the story so I can pay for the expedition.

I'm wearing my expedition boots in the airport. They are hot, but they were too big for the luggage. I have shoes in my carry-on that I can switch to when I get on the plane.

I need to sleep, but I need to watch my gear. I'll wait until I get on the plane.

Journal — 16 November 2013:

I'm wondering if there will be enough pages in this book. Just got on the plane for Santiago. Entering a world where I will be language disadvantaged. The LAN plane is very nice.

Journal — 17 November 2013:

Arrived in Punta Arenas. I'm staying at the hostel Vientos de la Patagonia. My luggage was so heavy. I'm now going through it and seeing what goes on the expedition and what stays behind.

Daniel Burton to Juan Menéndez — 17 November 2013:

Yes, I'm here but I'm not sure when my bike will get here.

Juan Menéndez complained his bike also hadn't arrived yet.

Daniel Burton to Juan Menéndez

11/17/13

Are you here? Did you get the bike?

Again, there was an email from Juan Menéndez with uncertain explanations. Daniel was being completely open about his own plans, but could not understand what Juan Menéndez was doing.

Daniel Burton's meditations when entering the city of Punta Arenas along the Strait of Magellan:

Blog — 17 November 2013:

Skipping winter

Well, I made it to Punta Arenas. It is about 9 pm but it is still light. Looks like I successfully skipped over winter.

I loved winter when I would ski, snowmobile, and do other winter sports. Skiing ended up becoming too expensive, and I opened a bike store and got to where I really didn't like winter. I would tell people I was ready for winter to end when the first snow storm hit. The fat bike changed that. Winter is still hard because sales at the store are low in the winter, but having a fun winter sport has brought the joy back into what otherwise would be a cold, dark season.

I talked to a couple of guys from the Czech Republic today. They are headed down to Union Glacier in a couple of days to do a marathon and a 100k run.

I got an email from Juan yesterday saying he is flying out, but doesn't have his bike. Not sure what that means."

Ten days were spent in Punta Arenas before the weather cleared enough to fly to Antarctica. Daniel's ten day layover in Chile narrowed the already small summer riding window in Antarctica.

Journal—19 November 2013

Someone wrote on a forum that my blog is like court-ordered community service. I think I need to make my blog entry shorter and more fun and make my full account here in my journal. I think part of the problem is that so far I am still just getting ready to leave. However, to some extent the expedition has begun yesterday walking along the beach. I started to feel a bit isolated. Since I don't speak Spanish and people here speak very little English, I don't talk to people much. I guess it is a good transition from the bike store where often I spend almost the whole day talking to people.

Journal—(More on) 19 November 2013:

Very happy and then very boring day. I walked down to the ALE office and they told me my bike arrived at the airport yesterday. They said they would go get it and give me a call at my hotel. I was so excited. I went back to my room and waited. No call. At three, I went to see if I could find the tours to Isla Magdalena. I misunderstood yesterday; the tour does not start at 5 PM. It is five hours long. It starts at 8 AM or 1 PM. So I think I will go to the 8 AM on Thursday. I'm a bit unhappy that I still have not gotten a call. When I go to the ALE place, they are nice, but it seems like they don't want to be bothered by me. It is frustrating that they said I was supposed to arrive five days before my departure, yet, so far, I have done nothing with them. I could've come a couple of days later and saved on hotel costs."

Journal—20 November 2013:

The hostel provides breakfast, which I eat at 8 AM each day. Today at 7:15 AM, I got a call saying my bike was here and they would meet me at 8:15 to go see it. I sneaked into the kitchen and ate a little and then went down to the ALE office and then to the warehouse where the bike is. I was happy to find everything in good shape. They built a box that kept the bike assembled and had just the bike in it. Everything else was in a bunch of small boxes.

The bad news is there is a $3,000 bill I have to pay for getting everything through customs and transported to Punta Arenas. I'm worried about running out of cash. Tracy Powell donated another $200 and the Richards have offered to help. Somehow, eventually, I need funds to be used to pay the loan instead of extra costs. I also bought some snowshoes and a tripod today. I ran out of room in my bags and figured it would be cheaper to buy those things than to pay for an extra bag. I spent most of the day putting everything into Ziploc bags. I initially wanted to vacuum pack everything, but the vacuum packer also did not fit. Hopefully, this turns out better because Ziploc bags allow me to reseal stuff and I have plenty of room in my sled.

One of the ALE guys said I should put skis under my sled. It may be too late to make changes. I met Doug Stoup who did an ice bike expedition over 10 years ago. He is working on an expedition by Toyota truck.

Overall, it was a great day, making good progress toward the start of biking.

Daniel Burton to Juan Menéndez 19 November 2013:

I worked on repackaging my food today. I just about have everything ready to go. I am in Hostel Vientos de la Patagonia just a few blocks from you. I am meeting at the ALE office tomorrow at 10.

Journal—21 November 2013:

I'm running out of power. I didn't bring stuff to charge from an outlet, just solar. I am in my room or in areas that just don't give me a chance to set up the solar panels, so my iPad and iPod are running out of power. Limping along on what solar power I can get.

A lot of people have asked if I am nervous. I would think by now the answer should be yes, but for some reason I am not. I think my mind is always busy trying to figure out what could go wrong and how to solve it. I think it just isn't giving my mind a chance to be nervous.

Preparing for the Willis Resilience expedition inside the Punta Arenas warehouse

Juan sin miedo

Talked with Juan today. He says he would like to cooperate, but he wants to be solo. I think if you cooperate, then it isn't solo. So I guess we are racing even though neither of us will say so. It would be so much easier if I didn't have to worry about him. He has a new untested bike, so, in that way, we are on similar ground. He wants a few days to get everything working right. I need to test my system and since we are not working together I think I need to not tell him when I will leave and just go when I can. I just wish I had a bit of a head start, but I was very open with my plan, which allowed him to push his schedule ahead so I don't get a head start.

I don't think yesterday's pizza helped. I haven't been doing a good job of eating enough. So yesterday, I went and got a pizza. I had to return to my room this morning to clean up after my guts rejected the pizza.

Daniel finally caught on that it was not wise to tell his competition all the details of his plan.

The story outside, "I fly down to Punta Arenas and get stuck there for an extra week waiting for the weather in Antarctica to get good enough to be able to fly to Union Glacier. I no longer have a hotel room so I stay with a Mormon bishop in Punta Arenas. He and his family don't speak English and I don't speak Spanish. I do a lot of drawing pictures on a white board to communicate with the Bishop."

Journal — 23 November 2013:

I bought a notepad so I now can write more here without worrying that I will run out of space. One of the great things about being LDS is you can go almost anywhere in the world and have instant friends. I got the address of the Bishop for the Ward that is in this area. I walked over to his house and knocked on the door. His wife answered the door to find some strange guy who doesn't speak Spanish. They don't speak English, but I was able to tell them that I'm Mormon and they called the missionaries. The Bishop offered to let me stay at his house while I wait for my flight. I know only some very basic words in Spanish and they know almost no English, so communicating is very hard. I used a white board to draw stick figures of my family and wrote down their ages. And then with some work we got my iPad connected to their Wi-Fi and then, using Google Translate and maps, was able to communicate a bit about who I am to them.

I don't have any decent clothes for church tomorrow, so I'll just have to go as I am.

Journal — 25 November 2013:

I was supposed to be in Antarctica by now, but delays for flights to Antarctica are common, so I am stuck in a waiting pattern, hoping for some good weather so we can fly down.

I went to church with the Bishop and family. It is a small Ward, only about 30 people, where they have two sets of missionaries—two elders and two sisters. The elders came over to the bishop's house for a family home evening yesterday. The sisters are coming tonight. The bishop's family was the only whole family I saw at church.

I walked down to the ALE office after church to let them know where I am. Mark wanted to drive out to the house so they would know how to find me. When we got there and saw the small humble home he said he thought bishops were rich with lots of rings and stuff. I told him that Mormon bishops were just members of the congregation and it was a volunteer nonpaid job. I need to walk down to the ALE offices again this morning to get a new status update.

Journal — 26 November 2013:

Still in Punta Arenas. They think MAYBE they can fly a resupply flight tomorrow. They have to fly fuel and supplies to the base camp before they can fly passengers. The weather looks like maybe tomorrow at 5 AM they can do the resupply, but then the weather looks bad again and the next flight probably won't be until Thursday or later. The katabatic winds are blowing from the south which is a good thing. If they take over the weather, the dry cold air will make it possible to fly. I walked for more than six hours today. Not much else to do while I wait. Maybe tomorrow I can find a penguin tour. I just want to start biking. Strong winds tonight. The Bishop's son is having pain in his side... maybe appendicitis. The Bishop is taking tomorrow off from work to watch his son. I think they are going by car somewhere to see the Penguins."

Daniel was stuck in a holding pattern. He would spend a total of ten days in Punta Arenas waiting for the weather to clear so they could fly to Antarctica. During those ten days, he got to know Punta Arenas well. With nothing much to do but wait, he would spend his days walking around the city, figuring that was the best way to stay in shape for the physically demanding expedition he was about to embark on. For the first five days, he stayed at a little hostel that was on the corner of the two streets in town where all the strip clubs were. When he headed out on his daily walks, he would be approached by people in the streets. Not understanding Spanish, he thought they were begging for money and eventually started avoiding the two strip club streets. It wasn't until later that he learned that the people on the street were not begging but trying to get him to go into the clubs.

27 NOV 13 1:15 AM

[The bishop's son] is still having problems with appendicitis. It seems strange to me that the doctors haven't given him any antibiotics.

I helped build a stable for their Christmas nativity set. We are getting better at communicating. They are learning some English and I am learning a bit of Spanish. It looks like maybe the weather in Antarctica was better today. Hopefully they were able to make the resupply flight. If so, maybe I can fly down tomorrow. I really need to start biking so I can finish and start taking care of my family.

Enough of this positioning. Let's do this. In December 2013, both Daniel Burton and Juan Menéndez begin bike expeditions to the South Pole.

The blue ice runway on Union Glacier

In Antarctica

Gone Forth to Look for Antarctica

Everybody knows that just getting to Antarctica by ship or by aircraft, from the end of either South America or Africa, over the terrifying Southern Sea is a courageous feat in itself.

Finally I am able to fly to Antarctica,

Daniel journaled.

When I get there I start testing out my bike setup. I haven't been able to test my setup before this because I didn't have any suitable conditions near my home and I knew if I was going to bike to the South Pole it had to be this year. While I am testing my biking setup, Juan spends his time testing his skiing setup. At this point I start to figure it will not be a bike race to the South Pole because he will ski part of the way.

No More Planning. Time to Go.

Anything you do in Antarctica can get you killed, including doing nothing. "I would have never made it to the South Pole if I hadn't ever tried. There were a lot of people that figured I should not try."

When you try something, people gather to watch you fail. Daniel reflected again on the message Mike Curiak had sent him on the Mountain Bike Review (Mtbr Forum): "My $.02 is that you are doing yourself (and those that would attempt it in the future) an enormous disservice by going from "nothing" to Antarctica. In other words, please, for your own good if no one else's, go somewhere else (Alaska, Norway, Greenland, NWT, wherever) and do a big, scary, push-your-limits shakedown ride (or three, or more) before moving forward on 'The Big One.' The point is to do your learning in a safer place, biting off bigger and bigger chunks before committing to something that, quite frankly, you do not and cannot grasp yet."

Another blog poster added, "Mike's advice is sound. It's way too dangerous/expensive of a trip to take on without at least some sort of serious winter touring experience. It would be smart to plan it out a few

Tent and bike at the base camp

years and gain experience in safer, more economically reasonable locales."

Of course they were right. An expedition to Antarctica was not a trivial thing, not a task to be taken lightly. Was Daniel making a big mistake? Was he in over his head? Or did he have what it would take? Only time would tell.

Journal—28 November 2013:

They finally were able to get the resupply flight in last night so maybe we can fly out tonight. I will find out in an hour or so. There is a late entry in the quest to be the first to bike to the South Pole. Some lady plans to fly to the South Pole, go by truck to a start location and ride a recumbent trike to the South Pole. She says she will start on December 10. Her route is half the distance [of mine], but I'm guessing more windy. By the time she flies down, gets to the pole, drives back to her start, and then starts biking, I hope to be most of the way there or even all the way there. We will see. If we fly out tonight, I need a little time to test my sled hitches and then I can start, so, hopefully, I'll be biking by December 1."

Mtbr Forum: another way to put it? Mistakes are the best teacher, and you... make as many as you can and embrace the lesson imparted by each. I don't think Antarctica is the place to do that."

Mtbr Forum: All of this talk begs the question: How can they be so-o-o sure that this trip is going to happen when funding (seemingly) hasn't been secured? I can't imagine how a person would find the means to do the trip on their own dime......and I can't imagine someone footing the bill given the current lack of info about their credentials."

Journal—29 November 2013:

Made it to Antarctica. The flight was a bit different. The jet is a Russian jet and is about what you would imagine a Russian military plane would be like on the inside. They had a dozen or so rows of seats with cargo behind. Because they are behind on flights, they packed the plane, which meant some people needed to sit on the military style benches. I volunteered. I was sitting with a big blue Arctic Trucks truck in my lap. The landing was interesting. They had a camera on the front of the plane and a big-screen TV to show as we approached the runway. First views of Antarctica were just as expected. Landing on ice was fun. As the plane touched down, the engines went into full reverse as usual, but, of course, there was no breaking from the wheels and steering seemed strange. Anyway, it took a lot of runway to come to a stop."

Mtbr Forum: I used the Colorado alpine as my main proving ground, then went to AK every February to put what I'd learned into practice. And you know what? No matter how many mistakes I made and lessons I learned, there was always another just around the corner.

Message of the Blog: "Everybody loves a fat bike...in Antarctica."

Blog 29 November 2013

My First Bike Ride in Antarctica

Distance 6.78 miles climb 187 feet descend 177 feet time 1:35

The first day in Antarctica has been great. We got here at about 4 in the morning Chile time which is the time zone I'll use for my expedition. That way the sun will be low in the south while I sleep and at my back while I travel.

After arriving I found a place for my tent and set up the minimums of camp and then got the bike put together. The bike was a big attraction at the base camp. I let anyone that wanted to take it for a test ride.

Everyone was surprised how light the Borealis bike is and how well it traveled on the snow.

It is kind of hot in the tent, but the outside weather is not that cold, I'm guessing around 20°F.

I took the bike out for a ride around the skiway (runway), about 6 miles. The bike did real well. However, no matter how hard you think it will be for me to bike to the South Pole...... It will be harder. I didn't have any weight on the bike and wasn't pulling a sled. I hear the conditions from Hercules to Patriot hills, about the first 30 miles, is very similar to the conditions here.

Daniel Burton prepared thoroughly...last minute rehearsal and inspection.

Blog 29 November 2013:

Second Test Ride

I did a second test ride today. 6.25 miles in 1'15". They have dinner at 7 and I left at 6 so I had to push hard to try and finish the ride in time. I ended up arriving at dinner late and soaked. They didn't have the heater on at dinner which is normally good, but I could have used the heat to dry off. After dinner I hung around trying to dry off and talking to people about the biking expeditions.

There are now three expeditions trying to be the first to bike to the pole, mine, Juan Menéndez Granados and some other lady that will try and do it with a recumbent fat trike. I don't want to use up all the minutes I got from the SatPhoneStore, so I don't have more details about her expedition. Anyway it will be interesting to see how this all works out.

After a while of hanging out after dinner, I was getting cold from being so wet. I went back to my tent, stripped down to my base layer and jumped in my sleeping bag. I wasn't in the bag for more than 10 seconds before I was toasty warm.

Tomorrow (actually it is just after midnight here so today) is the 1 year anniversary of my mom dying from high cholesterol. I was hoping to start my expedition on the 30th in honor of her, and to try and use this expedition to promote an active lifestyle. Of course promoting an active lifestyle will still be a goal for this expedition but I won't start going south until at least Dec 1. There are ski expeditions that are ahead of me for flying out.

Get out and do something.

The bike was a great hit with the staff and visitors at the base camp, but there was something wrong. Every once in a while when starting to pedal there would be a pinging noise. Was it the chain catching on the teeth of the gears? Was it something internal to the bottom bracket bearings? Or maybe something in the rear hub? It was a mystery that was starting to worry Daniel.

Journal—29 November 2013 12:57 pm:

Distance: 6.78 M. Ascent: 187. Descent: 177. 2 – 8 mph. 2: 27:56

I went for two bike rides today to test the bike. The first ride I kept relatively easy, but still got a bit wet from sweat. The second one I only had one hour to do the circuit, so I pushed hard and arrived at dinner soaked. It is cold in the tent now, so all the electronics are not

working. It was overly warm in the tent earlier. I'm going to take a nap and then decide what to do next."

Daniel could blog from Antarctica now. He blogged his experiences of the day with photographs and links. He journaled his thoughts and personal revelations at night in his tent out on the ice.

Blog—1 December 2013:

I rode today, but I didn't use a GPS so I don't know how far I went today. The weather all day has been cold and very windy. I figured it was a good chance to try less layers and see if it will still be warm enough. It was, but my toes got a bit cold, so I probably need to add back a layer on the pants. I also had big problems with goggles fogging up. I need to work on that. My wife asked if it was strange to have daylight 24 hours. Mostly no, but I always wake up every couple of hours at night and when it is so light it makes it seem like I have slept in. Then I look at my watch and realize I still need to sleep longer.

Dan wrote in his intimate confessional journal,

I think I have a sleeping disorder. Whenever I sit still for a few minutes I will fall asleep. Yet at night when I should be sleeping I wake every few hours or so. Usually I lie there for a few minutes and then go back to sleep. I rarely use an alarm to wake up in the morning as I wake often during the night and look at the clock to see what time it is and if I should get up. If I have something important that I need to get up early for I will set an alarm because if I don't I will wake up every 15 minutes and wonder if it is time to get up yet. I figured that my ability to sleep any time of the day would mean that sleeping in Antarctica would not be a problem. I was surprised that I actually had problems going to sleep at night.

It is now overcast and low visibility. None of the surrounding mountains are visible this morning. The wind also has picked up. It is a lot colder than yesterday. What was water in the bottom of my tent is now just ice.

At 11:00 I will get a route briefing. I will also pack my bags today and try and figure out the best way to distribute the load for this first segment. From the reports I have gotten the first 30 miles are going to be VERY hard.

In the dining building here at base camp they have an elevation profile for Hercules to South Pole. I have looked for this in the past but could never find one.

This is Antarctica!

I don't have any weather equipment. Just one of those extras that didn't make it. So I'm going to call this about a gazillion mph wind, and bitter cold. I have some of my food and my gas for the stove placed around the tent. It has all disappeared in the drifting snow. My tent is slowly getting buried.

Basically, if you think Antarctica is cold, wind, and inhospitable then you would not be disappointed in today's weather.

I had a route briefing today. We looked at the ground penetrating radar to see where crevasses are. We also looked at ice flow rates that help identify were crevasses are likely to be.

My route will start at Hercules inlet and climb up and around a big crevassed area and then basically go south with a bit of zig zagging to get around more dangerous areas. My route is a bit different than the ski routes so that it favors hard packed snow. However the first 30 miles will have a lot of soft snow and a lot of climbing.

At this meeting, Juan Menéndez got the ski routes as well as the bike routes from ALE. The planned route for skis took a short cut that would go more directly south, but would not have snow conditions as good as those of the bike route. When Daniel and Juan Menéndez got to the parting of the ways—since Juan Menéndez was skiing—he took the shortcut. Daniel recorded, "I was continuing on bike so I took the longer route. The biking between where we parted ways and where the paths rejoined was very difficult but with a lot of effort it was bikeable. Juan's blog states that he did not bike at all during his short cut, and for several days after the shortcut."

Blog—30 November 2013:

Dedicating Ride to My Mom

Well, I guess it is time to try riding in the worst blizzard you can imagine.

High cholesterol killed my mother one year ago today. I wanted to start riding south today but the weather isn't allowing me to get to the coast to my start. However I am still dedicating this expedition to her memory and using this as a way to encourage people to get out and be active.

I still have a few things I need to do before I can start biking to the pole. But the weather is so bad they can't fly out to the drop off point and with a couple of ski expeditions ahead of me it will be a couple of days before I can start so there isn't a lot of pressure to dig my gear out of the snow drift it has disappeared into and get things finalized.

With the strong wind and blowing snow I figured it was a good time to try out layering options. I dropped a couple of layers out of what I have been wearing and still was plenty warm.
I had problems with my goggles fogging up and not being able to tell where I was going. I will work on a couple of ideas to see if I can fix this problem.

I thought I could get distance info from my inReach but it doesn't give me that info so I don't know how many miles I did today but it was only about an hour of riding.

My tent is slowly turning into an igloo, it is cold and windy but it is awesome to be in Antarctica.

Blog — 1 December 2013:

Ready to start

The ski expeditions to the South Pole are scheduled to fly out today. That means that they should be able to fly me to my start soon. I tested pulling two sleds with full panniers. It worked better than I expected. The weight in the panniers[11] helps. Without the panniers I spin out in the softer snow, but with the panniers I don't have that problem.

I filled my hydro flask with hot chocolate before I left on the ride today and when I stopped for a drink it was gone. I was afraid I had lost it somewhere but when I got back to camp it was waiting for me. I filled it with hot water a couple of days ago when it was even colder out. I did

---

[11] On the harder packed snow at base camp the panniers did help some with traction, but lowering the air pressure in the tires turned out to be a better way to get traction.

my bike ride and then forgot about it and left it out in the blizzard overnight. I was worried that maybe the contents would be frozen and my bottle would be damaged. But after all night in a raging blizzard the contents were still nice and warm.

It seems all my equipment is working as good or better than I expected except for my Sherpa 50. For some reason I can't get it to charge.[12] I figured a 110 charger would be of no use on this trip but there is power at the dinner tent, so I wish I had my 110 charger to see if that would charge it.

Journal — 1 December 2013:

I did a poor job of remembering the Sabbath Day. It was halfway through the day before I realized it was Sunday. After that I tried to keep it a holy day of rest and have my own little sacrament meeting.

On the Mtbr Forum:

Please give it some thought. I'd like to see the next group succeed, instead of just provide more no-room-for-private-expeditions fodder for the NSF (United States National Science Foundation) and others of their ilk.

Dan, blogging:

I am all ready to go now. I just need a flight. I tested my stove to melt water for my sacrament. I thought my Sherpa wasn't charging, but it is now about 50% charged. It just needed more sunlight. Hopefully, by the time I wake in the morning it will be charged. I'm a messy camper."

Mtbr Forum:

Saying that this is the first time a bike has been ridden to the South Pole before it has actually been done seems a bit odd. It has been attempted before and you will be attempting to do so again.

"I received a lot of criticism for talking as if it was a forgone conclusion that I would be successful. People viewed it as an arrogant attitude, but I was working on my mental toughness training. I had to

---

[12] Li-ion batteries do not work well in cold conditions. The Sherpa 50 did not work well in Antarctica, and I thought it was broken. When I got home, I gave it to Goal Zero to look at. They were able to get it to recharge, and it has worked fine since.

train my mind to believe I would finish or there would be no way I could do it. Mahatma Gandhi said,

> Man often becomes what he believes himself to be. If I keep on saying to myself that I cannot do a certain thing, it is possible that I may end by really becoming incapable of doing it. On the contrary, if I have the belief that I can do it, I shall surely acquire the capacity to do it even if I may not have it at the beginning.

Flying to Hercules Inlet

On your mark. Get set. Go!

On Dec. 2, 2013, Burton arrived at Hercules Inlet with hundreds of thousands of pedal cranks ahead of him. The first one was the easiest — it all went downhill (figuratively speaking,) from there in his trek to the most southern spot on earth.

Blog — 2 December 2013:

The Fun Begins

55 min .89 miles total ascent 93 feet total descent 16 feet elevation 1266 temp in tent 64.8.

Finally I am biking to the South Pole. I flew out of base camp at about 6pm to Hercules inlet. There is a cache of supplies there for Richard Park. He is trying to set the unassisted, unsupported record from Hercules to the South Pole, but he ran into bad weather, so he is on his way back to the start. It may be that I will see him on his way to Hercules and then again as he passes me on his second attempt.

Juan is still at base camp. I'm not sure if he will try and pass me or not. He has skis and I've been told he plans to put his bike on the sled and ski in the deep snow. That should be a lot faster than my hike-a-bike method. My goal is to never put my bike in the sled.

Daniel was able to achieve this goal.

The snow in Hercules inlet was soft making travel difficult, but that was what I was expecting. Just outside the inlet is a steep climb. It is a sea of white waves of drifted snow with just a few tops of mountains showing like little islands. With the look of being out to sea, the steepness is hidden from the eyes, but when trying to pull a couple hundred pounds of gear up the slope, there is no doubt that you are climbing.

I was hoping to clear the top of the first slope today, but I started to worry I left my camera at the start, so I set up camp, and in the process found the camera.

Tomorrow will be my first full day of biking to the pole.

"The plan was to bicycle 750 miles in 50 days. I really thought I would be done in 20 to 30 days but had 50 days of food just in case," he wrote. "I'm thankful for the experience of others." If Daniel hadn't made his contingency plan that reflected the experience of the serious ones, the great ones, he would not have made it to the South Pole.

Daniel planned for what he knew and what he did not know. He knew he would start out at sea level and end on the Pole at 9,300 feet above sea level.

The blog is starting to feel like...this is getting real.

A funny thing happened on the way to the South Pole.

Blog:

Max speed—4.4 Ascent—1836 Descent—1074 Elevation—2023 Distance 6.26—Time 9:25

I was told that elevation from a barometer doesn't work in Antarctica. These numbers seem to prove that true. There was 0 descent. The whole day was climbing and steeper climbing. With the soft snow and the weight of my gear, and of course uphill into a head wind, those miles were harder than could possibly be explained.[13]

That seriously was the hardest six miles I have ever done. I will be so glad when I get to the polar plateau and things level off a bit. In another 22 miles it is supposed to get better.

Daniel knew he would push against headwinds the whole way. He did *not* know he would literally "face" *katabatic* winds that would blow him to a stop, standing on his pedals, unable to make them go around. The usual winds were 10–20 mph, but 20–40 mph was possible. More than 20 mph was rare, but Murphy's Antarctic Law says that if it is rare for everybody else, it is inevitable for you.

Daniel would find that, even though he pedaled for thirteen to fourteen hours per day, he wasn't keeping up with the schedule. He was supposed to make twelve to fourteen miles every day, but he had many days of five to six miles progress. Once, he had only made two miles into the fierce, "ice-sand storm" wind. He had to do better. He had to find a way to keep to the average the schedule demanded. His best day was 24 miles.

Imagine bicycling along and in a split second being bludgeoned with a hurricane force gust of wind so powerful that it simply stops your forward progress. Your puny weight standing on the pedals cannot move you. Then add to that an ambient temperature below zero with a (hurricane feeling) wind chill that plunges the windchill temperature on your body to 70 or 90 below zero. Of course, this wind in your face is full of thousands of granules of ice that would stab you like 10,000 pins. The only way to survive this was to make sure that absolutely no skin was exposed. This meant a mask over the face and the strong wind would press the mask against the nose and mouth making it difficult to breath. Oh, and you are trying to go uphill…with panniers full of supplies draped on your bike. Lastly, you drag behind you not one but two sleds full of precious food and camp equipment that is the only thing between you and death when you finally give up and stop for the "night."

---

[13] In June 2014 Daniel went for a bike ride with his son and a friend, Jake. They climbed up to the ridge line at 9,600 feet between Utah, Salt Lake, and Wasatch counties. At one point, Jake commented about it being the hardest six miles he had ever done. Daniel could not help to think that it was not nearly as hard as the easiest six miles of Antarctica.

After a day of that, Daniel was exhausted. His expedition seemed impossible. He couldn't make five miles a day in a true katabatic storm, let alone thirteen. But he was an optimist and his hopefulness would not desert him ("There is hope smiling brightly before us and we know that deliverance is nigh" went the hymn he remembered from church). He camped. He slept. He ate and drank. The wind died. ("The wind and the waves shall obey thy will. Peace; be still.") He could go on. He could find a way.

More 3 December Journal:

I got dropped off late. I have to call in to my support at 9:40 PM each day, so it was a short day. I thought about just calling in and making a longer day, but, at about 8 PM, I had this fear that I had left my camera at the start, so I set up camp and went through all my gear and found the camera. It was nice to not have to do yesterday's miles 2.5 times. When I got dropped off, they wanted to get pictures, so I spent a bit of time riding in the ski track from the plane. That worked well, but off the ski track I couldn't ride much at all even though I didn't have any of the gear on the bike.

Mtbr Forum:

"It's a tough enough ride without having to sort out your gear and winter riding techniques on the fly."

Daniel journals on:

After the plane left, I split my gear a bit into two loads and hooked up my rear axle mounts. Then I could put the panniers on. It is a heavy load. I had to walk the first part because it was so soft, but after a while, I found a spot I could get on and ride. I made good speed on the bike but not for long. There is a good slope after the edge of the inlet. When I hit that, the snow got harder. It looked level because all you can see is a sea of white, so the slope hides itself. I thought I should be able to get on the bike and ride, but I just couldn't pull the load up the hill. I then tried leaving one sled, thinking maybe I would pull half the load and then go back and get the other half. I couldn't even pull half the load up the hill, so I hooked up both sleds and just pushed the bike. It was hard work and I was drenched in sweat, which is dangerous, but the required effort to move even very slowly was hard and there was no way to not sweat. It was sunny and a bit of a tailwind so not too cold so I didn't get cold from all the sweat. I am reorganizing my gear. I'm going to put all the food on one sled and gear on the other. I used hot water from the base camp and made up stew and breakfast. I ate about half the stew last night, so I haven't fired up the stove yet. I'll eat breakfast and start moving and melt my first snow tonight.

Get going early. Pedal all day. Repeat for 51 days.

For the first few days, Burton rode on his Borealis fat bike. Even a five-inch tire mounted on a 26-inch wheel struggled in the soft snow and headwinds Burton encountered. Pulling a 150-pound sled loaded with supplies through soft snow in perpetual ascension toward the polar plateau, he prayed things would "level off a bit." He cranked onward day after day, averaging only six miles per day for the first week. Daniel Burton knew when he left that his epic journey was going to be difficult, but nothing could prepare him for the welcome Antarctica had in store.

"I start my expedition on December 2. On December 3 I fall into a crevasse."

Daniel explains the photo he took, blog:

This may be hard to see and understand, but the hole just left of the sled is the crevasse I fell into. The scary thing about this picture is that without the hole you would never know that this is a snow bridge across a crevasse.

How big and deep is this crevasse? I don't know. I wanted to go back and get a better picture, but I was too scared to get any closer to it. Also interesting in this picture is the number of ski tracks going over the crevasse. All the other expeditions skied over this crevasse without even knowing it was there. In fact Richard Park skied over this just about 30 minutes before I fell into it."

Later Juan passes me. He is on his skis and I am mostly pushing my bike and riding when I can. For the first 30 miles I get about 6 miles a day, but figure when I get to the resupply route that ALE uses that things will get better. The wind, climbing, and soft snow make travel very difficult for me. By the time I get up to the route ALE is using, the tracks from their last resupply are old and filled in with soft snow drifts, and I fail to get any faster. At this point I figure I will not make it to the South Pole before I run out of time. When I call my wife on the sat phone I tell her I will keep going until I run out of time.

Crevasse

Journal — 3 December 2013:

Max speed 4.4 total ascent 1836 Descent 1074 Elevation 2023 Distance 6.26 Time 9:25

I got an early start today. I just haven't been tired so I haven't slept a lot. Maybe I took too many naps while waiting in Punta Arenas. The hill I was climbing yesterday got steeper and steeper. I could barely push the bike up at the end of the hill, but after that hill came another that was just as bad as the first. Then I ran into Richard Park who was trying to set a speed record but wasn't going to make it so he is headed back to the start so he can try again. Climbing these hills once is more than enough for me.

Mtbr Forum:

I'm glad he has satellite comms so he can call on help as needed.

They are still convinced that there is no way Daniel can do this and sooner or later he will have to call in to be rescued. That however was an option that would never enter into his mind.

> Just after I left Richard, I stepped into a crevasse. It was a bit scary. I was pushing the bike when my right foot broke through. I wasn't in any danger of falling in, at least I don't think I was. I got out and onto some blue ice I figured was safe and then looked back. I wanted to look into the hole to see how big it was, but I didn't dare step off the piece of ice I was on.

> As time went on, my left knee started to have a little pain. I was tired from working so hard and just couldn't push anymore, so I quit after nine hours and 25 minutes. Maybe I'll sleep tonight.

Blog—4 December 2013:

> **50**

> Happy birthday to me. The day started out windy with more soft snow and climbing. I am not making the distances I would like. Today was 6.2 nautical miles. With 10.5 hours.

> Juan skied past me today. His travel by ski is at least three times faster than my combo hike-a-bike and riding. After he passed he set up his tent. It seemed strange that he would end the day so soon, but maybe it was for a different reason, because as soon as I caught up with him he took his tent down and skied off into the horizon.

> The slope isn't as steep now and the snow is harder. I dropped the air pressure down as low as possible in the tires and can now ride for longer distances, but it is still hard and uses a lot of energy.

Daniel's prediction that Juan would be skiing and not biking was right. Juan Menéndez wrote in his blog that he did not bike for the first ten days. Meanwhile, Daniel was riding his bike for a few feet, getting stuck in soft snow, and then he would need to wait a minute or two to allow his heart to recover before he could push his bike out of the snow drift. Then he would get back on his bike and ride a few more feet before hitting the next snow drift.

Journal—5 December 2013 am:

> I didn't get out of the tent early enough. It was calm, but now the wind has picked up so I have to pack everything up in the wind.

I'm not going to repeat what I said on the voice recorder so I'll just end now.

Journal — 5 December 2013 pm:

A bit discouraged today. I only went for seven hours and got 4.7 miles. The snow is soft and drifted and the wind is unbearably strong and the slope is too steep for the weight and sleds I'm pulling. It is 10 miles to the route where it is supposed to be packed from travel and not as steep. At the rate I've been going it would take two days to get there, but I'm hoping to start early tomorrow and make the full 10 miles.

Blog — 5 December 2013:

Katabatic Winds!

Been fighting a strong katabatic wind today. It finally just got to be too much, and I needed to add another layer so I put up the tent. I'm getting good at setting up and taking down the tent in strong winds. The first thing I do is attach the tent to a sled or the bike so it won't blow away. Today I attached it to the bike and the tent was dragging the bike until I got a couple of stakes into the snow.

Saw Juan again today. He was in the distance taking down his tent and then he skied off. I imagine that is the last time I will see him. I don't think he has ridden his bike yet.

While alternating between riding and hike-a-bike the Saratoga Farms Pasta Alfredo I had seen in the morning was calling out to me. Eating it now and it is even better than I had hoped. I'm hoping the winds die down tonight. If they do I'll be all refueled and ready to go.

I only got 7 hours in so far today, and I don't know how many miles because the GPS is still out on the bike ticking away minutes, but I am not motivated enough to put a coat back on and go get it. Besides the fur ruff is just starting to thaw out.

Blog — 6 December 2013:

Over the Hill

I am probably the most excited 50 year old to be over the hill but I am so glad to have finished what should be the hardest part.

After ending early yesterday because of the wind I started early this morning with the goal to hit the waypoint on the route they use to supply the ski way. I barely made it in time to finish riding and make my call to ALE.

I tried several different things with the bike configuration and was able to do a lot more riding today. Still the hike-a-bike is easier, but starting tomorrow the conditions should be better for biking.

Sunny and light winds today. 12 nautical miles.

Daniel had worked very hard to get that 12 miles and make it over the hill. When he called in to ALE to report his hours he told them 18 hours, but in reality it was longer than that. The voice on the other end of the satellite phone seemed unsure of the number of hours reported, so Daniel changed his report to 15 hours to make it sound more reasonable. Taking more than 18 hours to travel 12 miles was not a good sign. It was starting to look like there would be no way Daniel would be able to reach the pole in time. Daniel, however, was convinced that things would improve and he would be able to increase his speed and get more miles in future days.

Nautical miles? Lat Longs? Knots to it!

Journal—7 December 2013 am:

I made it! I got the 10 (nautical) miles and made it to the resupply route. It doesn't seem as packed as I thought it would be, but I will find out more when I start riding. Yesterday I got going real early... 4:30 maybe. For the first 3 miles I tried my method of pulling one sled by hand and then pulling the other by bike. It involved three times the distance, and after spending so long to get 3 miles on easier terrain than what I was doing before, I decided it was stupid, so I hooked both sleds back to the bike and pulled. This meant the last 7 miles were all done hike-a-bike whereas with just one sled I could pull it with the bike most of the time. I'm trying to lighten my load by eating as much as possible and adding orange mix or hot chocolate to the water to use it up. I think it is helping. I don't know how well I will be able to travel the resupply route, but I am hoping for 24 miles a day.

"24 miles a day? Man, I was optimistic."

First cache at S 82 29.720 W 079 28.429

What do those letters and numbers mean? They mean that Daniel was recording that his first cache was at 82 degrees and 29.72 minutes of south latitude and 79 degrees, 28.429 minutes of west longitude. An English statute mile is 5,280 English feet. Therefore, on land, one mile per hour is 5,280 feet per hour. But a Nautical mile is 6,076.12 English feet. 6,076.12 feet was chosen because that distance equals one "minute" of arc around the 360 degrees of the circumference of the globe. So, 60 minutes equals 60 nautical miles. 60 minutes also equals one degree of arc over the surface of the earth. And so there are 60 nautical miles per degree. There are 360 degrees around the circumference of the earth, be it around the poles or around the equator (well, pretty much. This old earth bulges a little in the middle, like many people that don't get out and exercise). So, the earth is 60 times 360 nautical miles around its circumference. This is a total of just over 21,600 nautical miles. But, the reader asks, I was taught the world is a little more than 25,000 miles around the whole circle. Ah, but that is in *statute* miles. Nautical miles are longer and so there are fewer of them in a given distance.

So, when Daniel says he wants to go 24 nautical miles in 13.5 hours, he is saying he wants to keep to a pace or a rate of two knots. What does that mean? It means he wants to go two nautical miles per hour. Why "knots?" This is because, in the old days of sailing ships, the sailors would toss a block of very buoyant wood overboard tied to a thin light twine with knots tied in it every 47 feet. Simultaneously, the sailors would start a thirty second sand glass. When the sand ran through the glass, the sailor letting the twine pay out over the side would pinch it and see how many *knots* in the twine had paid out over the water. Each knot that went over the side represented one nautical mile per hour. (If you wish it, the mathematical formula for "knots" is certainly available). The total number of knots paid out over the side equaled the speed of the ship in nautical miles per hour...hence Daniel wants to bike over Antarctica at a consistent average of two knots.

But why would Daniel use nautical miles on land? Because Antarctica can be thought of as a huge continental glacier. Just as a glacier is a frozen river which still flows, however slowly, so can Antarctica be considered a frozen sea with frozen waves and katabatic swept currents. So, Antarctic explorers have always used nautical navigation...degrees, minutes, and seconds of longitude and latitude and nautical miles per hour – knots (KTS).

Daniel had the goal and the requirement to travel from 80° south latitude (degrees of arc south from the equator) at Hercules Inlet to 90° south latitude at the South Pole (Has to be 90°, right? Because from the

equator to the Pole is one fourth of the circle of the earth which is 90°).
This is a total of ten degrees. Ten degrees is 600 nautical miles or about
733 statute miles. However, his route would not be in a straight line south
so his final mileage would end up being 775 miles. This was the distance
Daniel had to bicycle carrying his panniers and dragging his pulkas
through four food caches before the winter arrived at and the people left
from the South Pole.

Blog — 7 December 2013:

Interval Training

15.5 miles

Now that it is more level and I am following the Thiel Mountain
resupply route. Travel is a lot easier, but that does not mean it is easy.
There are a lot of new soft snow drifts with occasional hard snow. In
order to keep pedaling I go as slowly and easily as I can, but frequently
'as slowly and easily as possible' means a full out effort. So it is a lot like
doing intervals of all out effort followed by short recoveries. Of course,
there are some drifts that are too soft and too big so I have to push out
of those.

I thought the sleds being too heavy was a problem and of course it is. So I moved as much weight as possible from the sleds to the panniers. It made it worse. So I put as little weight as possible in the panniers and that works much better.

I am running with very little pressure in the tires. I sometimes worry that it will pinch flat, but it gives me the float I need. In all my messing around with the load I left my shovel behind, TWICE. What an idiot! So I traveled 3 times as far as how much I actually progressed towards the pole. However, now I have things figured out, so I think it will be better going forward. Except a wind storm has moved in and they say it will continue until Monday.

I am back on the same route the skiers are using. The ski tracks do harden the snow a bit but not nearly as well as bike tracks do. Unfortunately for me there are only ski tracks on the ground.

Juan Menéndez had rejoined Daniel's route at this point. From following his track before the parting of ways, Daniel could tell Juan Menéndez's ski tracks by the way his sled pulled to one side, and by the distinctive marks that his ski poles made.

Mtbr Forum:

Also, don't get me wrong: I wish you nothing but success...... I just think you could dramatically improve your odds by taking advice from those with experience doing the type of thing you're hoping to do.

Blog—8 December 2013:

Happy Birthday Mike

'And the evening and the morning were the first day.'

Well, it is never evening, morning, or night here, only day. So I guess I am still on the first day. Being the Sabbath, I tried to take it easy today. However, nothing about this trip is easy. The day started out with high winds so I added my Pearl Izumi barrier pants and jacket. It worked well. The winds create a lot of soft drifted snow that makes biking very hard. At least though it has gotten to the point that biking is better than hike-a-biking.

I got a bit of a late start this morning, biked about 5 hours, set up my tent, fixed lunch, and then continued biking. I figure I was biking to church, but I never found a chapel ;-)

I really need to start getting in more miles per day. My sleds are just too heavy. I worked with a few different setups and should be able to start doing better tomorrow.

Journal — 8 December 2013:

> Didn't get 24. In fact, towards the pole only five. I changed my load to add weight to the panniers instead of the sled; it made it worse. Then I moved my load to the sled and discovered I left the shovel at the last place I changed the load. So I rode back and got the shovel, but left it at this new location. When I got to the five hour mark I set up my tent and there was no shovel, so I went back and got it again. Once was bad enough, but twice is just stupid. I did have fun riding back the first time. After a path is packed down the bike travels well. I think we need a 24-hour Antarctica race. Hoping to do better today while trying to remember it is the Sabbath day.

Blog — 9 December 2013:

Viento Blanco

I got a nice early start today. Planning to ride 5-6 hours, take a break and go another 5-6 hours.

I started making good time. It was hard going but I thought I would get my first good mileage day. The winds kept getting stronger and stronger. It was hard to stand let alone bike or push into the wind. But setting up the tent in this wind didn't sound fun either. It finally got to the point that no matter how hard I pushed I couldn't move forward. So now I'm in the tent eating freeze dried mangos and waiting for it to get back down to something like 30 mph so I can go again.

Writing, spirits, and attitude starting to wear down.

Journal — 10 December 2013:

Well, so far I have not been getting the number of miles a day I need to be successful. It was really windy yesterday and I only rode for about two hours. It was windy again this morning (and all night) so I didn't start riding until noon. I got eight hours in and 8 miles. I will go again after I eat and do my scheduled call in. I know that I need to be getting in the upper teens each day and I have yet to do that. As I eat stuff and get my sleds lighter it helps also that I'm getting better at having my clothing working and not stopping every few seconds to adjust stuff. So, I hope I can start improving at this point. It looks like I won't reach the pole. Maybe it will get better, but whatever happens, I will go on as long as I can.

Daniel says, "This really was the low point in my expedition. I called my wife on the satellite phone and informed her that I most likely would not make it to the South Pole. She agreed with me that I should continue going south and see how far I could go. Strangely, I had now been biking about the same number of days that the highly experienced Eric Larsen spent biking towards the South Pole before he turned around."

Mtbr Forum:

I really think the odds are against Daniel due to his major lack of experience. Some of the posts I've seen by him are just comical. I get the impression he is really clueless about what he is taking on, BUT I have to hand it to the guy, he is still going after a few days, learning what he probably should have learned after a few years of research and training. Regardless of whether he makes it, I give him major props for being out there for this long with his lack of experience. I just hope he is prepared for the whole thing to be difficult and slow going and sticks it out.

The cruelty of Antarctica.

Blog—10 December 2013

Boot To The Head

15.3 nautical miles

Finally a day that I travelled enough miles to be able to be successful. If I can average 15nm a day from here on out I should make it. The snow drifts from the recent wind have started to get hard making travel easier. Sometimes I can even go a whole mile without stopping.

The cruelty of Antarctica is, the steeper the slope, the softer and larger the snow drifts. Some years ago after completing my second Brianhead Epic I told my kids that if I ever said I wanted to do that again they should take a 2x4 and smack me upside the head. They have been hoping I will do it again ever since. Luckily for me they no longer do the Brianhead Epic. However, doing the South Pole Epic is worse than doing the Brianhead Epic, day after day.

I can't do a 10 hour day without breaking it up. I get too hungry and it is just too hard to eat while biking. So I am now doing two 5 hour shifts a day. Set up the tent in between and get a good meal. Also this way I only need to drag around 5 hours of water at a time.

Looking back Daniel said, "This was a great plan, but most days I would find I just was not getting enough miles, so I would skip my midday break and keep biking. Eventually I gave up on the idea of stopping mid-day."

Blog—11 December 2013:

Juan Carlos, Layne, and Todd

15 nm today! I was told that that was the most miles for any of the expeditions today. Probably because the other expeditions are further south and they have more uphill. The snow keeps getting better. I can now bike over snow drifts that just yesterday were soft and extremely difficult to push over. Even though the conditions get easier, my work load remains the same; I just get more distance.

The mountain in Provo has a big Y on it for BYU. There is a U in Salt Lake City for the University of Utah, and a G in Pleasant Grove for their high school. When I was a teenager they wanted to name a new high school Lincoln. We joked that then they could put up an L and the mountains would spell "ugly." Anyway, when Juan Carlos [not Menéndez but Luciani], Layne, and Todd were getting me into mountain biking (there were many others, but those three were the ones that pushed me the most) we would bike to the top of the Y. The challenge was to make it the whole way without putting a foot down. It involved biking at near max effort the whole way, but somehow you had to learn to recover while climbing. I only made it the whole way without stopping once before they closed the trail to bikes.

Biking to the South Pole is like climbing the Y for 5 straight hours, taking a break and then doing it again for 5 more hours. I am constantly near my max effort, yet have to find a way to recover while working, and keep going. I eventually get stuck and have to stop. Maybe someday I will be able to get a full mile in before getting stopped. For now I am just happy that I actually got 3 sessions in a row that look like it may be possible to reach the end goal.

Chicken Teriyaki with Rice for dinner tonight.

Daniel was getting good at his regular routine. When it was time to stop for the day, he would find a suitable place to set up the tent. Frequently, he would try to set up his tent in a place that would have a fun GPS location—at least to a nerd—like an even latitude, or a latitude with repeating numbers. Because there was a constant wind out of the south, he would secure the tent by attaching the head rope to his bike before removing anything from his sleds. Then he could safely remove the tent from the sleds. The wind would catch the tent and lay it out for him. This meant that the head of his tent was always at the south with the foot and vestibule facing north.

Daniel had purchased a Hilleberg Nammatj 2. This was a great tent for South Pole expeditions because it was light yet strong. It was an excellent four season tent with a large vestibule. The vestibule was used as a kitchen and a place to store the sleds while he slept. The vestibule also provided plenty of room to work on the bike.

The tent had been modified with flaps sewn to the bottom of the outer tent. After pitching the tent, Daniel would use a shovel to cover the flaps with snow. This served two purposes: it secured the tent so it would not blow away in the wind, and it kept cold air from blowing under the outer tent, helping to keep it warm inside.

After the tent was set up, Daniel would bring his sleds into the vestibule where he could access them without having to leave the warmth and wind protection provided by the tent.

The next task was to lay down a Therma-Rest pad, and then inflate an Exped DownMat and place it on top of the Therma-Rest. This was topped off with a Marmot CWM sleeping bag.

Next, Daniel would select a meal for the evening, and set up his MSR Whisper International stove in the vestibule. Daniel could close the door between the main tent and the vestibule to protect against carbon monoxide poising.

Antarctica is technically a desert, but there is plenty of water in the form of ice. Daniel would scoop up snow from the south west corner of the vestibule and fill a pot. This would provide the water needed for drinking and to rehydrate the freeze dried meals. The funny thing was that the large hole left behind from getting ice for water was always in the same place. Yet in spite of his best efforts, most days he would fall into the hole while taking down the tent the next morning.

After eating a nice meal, Daniel would make a phone call to ALE to inform them where he was and how far and how long he had traveled. Frequently this phone call was followed by a call to his wife. Then he would create a blog post and upload it using the satellite phone and RedPort Optimizer that SatPhoneStore had provided him. This allowed him to connect his iPod and iPad via WiFi to the internet.

All of Daniel's clothing, gloves, jacket, jerseys, pants, and socks would need to be dried while he slept. The solar radiation not only warmed the tent, but would do a good job of drying everything out. Everything was laid out in the tent or hung from ropes at the top of the tent for drying.

After writing an entry in his journal, Daniel would try to get some sleep. The 24 hours of daylight and biking hard all day frequently made it hard for him to get to sleep. Biking for an average of 13 hours a day meant that in order to get eight hours of sleep his evening and morning routines needed to be completed in less than three hours. Usually the evening and morning tasks took more than three hours, which meant he did not get enough sleep.

Blog — 12 December 2013:

One of Those Days

I knew going into this that there would be days when I just didn't want to do this. This morning was one of those. I slept in. It was nice and warm in my sleeping bag and I just didn't want to go out into the cold. I ended up starting hours later than I had planned. And then I just had no motivation to go hard on the bike, and that is the only option because there is no easy on this expedition. After a while I got back into expedition mode, and the rest of the day went well.

The ski tracks I have been following have been covered in snow drifts. Then today I started to notice that they were no longer covered in drifts and look nice and fresh. This means they were created after the big wind storm a few days ago. This gave me hope that I was on track for completing the expedition. Also I got another 15.1 nautical miles in today which is a number that works well.

Big milestone of the day, I completed my first degree! I stopped for a minute at 81° south and celebrated with a drink of weak chocolate water and a pink Honey Stinger waffle and then continued on. Only 9 more degrees to go, and that first degree was the tough one because of the climb out of Hercules Inlet and having to go around the big crevasse field. There are still a few crevasses I have to go around but mostly from here on it is headed south. So at 15 nautical miles a day that is 4 days per degree and I should be able to arrive at the pole before the end of the season.

Back home in Utah my father was closely following my progress, and he was also calculating the distance. Based on his calculations he figured I was still not getting enough mileage.

Journal — 12 December 2013 am:

I've messed up today. I was supposed to start biking by three and it is now almost 7. I need to get going, but the sleeping bag felt so good. It was hard to get up and out into the cold and get going. In spite of my efforts everything is not dry yet.

Journal — 12 December 2013 pm:

I write in my blog. Sometimes I record with my voice recorder and sometimes I make little videos and then, of course, there is this Journal. Sometimes I don't know what to write that is not a repeat of what I have written elsewhere. I slept in this morning. It worked out well. I think I will try to do tomorrow's schedule like today was if I'm on the bike before eight and then again before three then I can get two five hour sessions which gets me good results. When I have had enough sleep that seems to be when I have dreams. What do you dream about when on an expedition? This morning it was climbing Kings Peak with my cousin James. The strange thing is he doesn't like camping and the mountains in my dream looked nothing like Kings Peak. The other day I had a strange dream that, with the right mental powers, people could pass through walls. It was weird. People were using it for a theft ring and then I learned how to pass through walls and used that ability to work against the theft ring. Strange stuff. Well, hopefully, I can get enough sleep tonight.

Daniel says, "Looking back, I am surprised that I was only doing ten hours or less of travel per day up to this point. Later I would do 13 hours most days and some days more. I think this is because I had read expedition logs, and got the impression that 10 hours was a long day for an expedition, but for me it was not enough to get the distances I wanted."

Juan Menéndez and Daniel would actually race to the Pole, side by side, glimpsing each other across the blazing white ice, but what was the Spaniard doing over there, really? Juan Menéndez Granados may or may not have been qualifying for the competition or the title. The way was still open for Daniel to claim that title, except for…

Where is Juan?

12 December 2013 continued:

I have been following Juan's ski tracks and they have been covered by snow drifts. Today, they started looking fresh. I decided that meant that I had gotten at least as far as he had when the last big windstorm hit. Then I found a campsite and the tracks from there on looked like they had to have been made today. So maybe I am only a day behind him. There have been no bike tracks, so even though it is now very bikeable, it looks like Juan is still doing it by ski.

Mtbr Forum:

I would agree with you that he doesn't have the cold weather and snow riding experience to make this a successful effort. An interview with his wife and son was very telling to me.

Blog — 13 December 2013:

Friday the 13th? No Wonder!

Woke up and could tell that it was cloudy but not too windy. I'm thinking this will be a great day, but after getting the tent all packed up I discovered I could not see any details in the snow. I could not tell where the route went and had a hard time seeing the ski tracks. It is important that I stay on the packed trail or it gets real hard to move. I kept losing the trail and having to search for it. Following a compass would work, but would not keep me on the packed route. So instead of being a great day I was creeping along.

At lunch time I decided to give up my midday break so that at least I would get a reasonable number of miles in by adding 2 hours to my travel time. Then finally in the afternoon the lighting changed. I was able to ride at a pretty good clip much of the time and was able to salvage the day with my third 15 nautical mile day... 15.1 actually. That gives me a quarter of a degree a day.

All in all it was a very, very difficult day, but then so was every other day. The first time I completed LOTOJA,[14] as I crossed the finish line I said, "Get me off this bike!" I guess the people running the finish line thought it was a call for help and they came running up to keep me from falling over. I was tired, but not that tired. Today I needed those people to come and catch me. Several times I would be so exhausted I could not hold my balance and would fall over.

Todd tried to talk me into doing the 'Race Across America.' I was pretty close to being talked into it until the last time I did LOTOJA. After finishing and walking to the car I thought, "There is no way I want to do this again tomorrow." Well, every day of this expedition is harder than

---

[14] LOTOJA is the LOgan TO JAckson race, the longest United States Cycling Federation (USCF) sanctioned one day bike race in America. It starts in Logan, Utah and goes 206 miles to Jackson Hole, Wyoming. It is the iconic long endurance race for bikers in Utah. Daniel did LOTOJA six times, which is a large part of what got him physically ready for the South Pole.

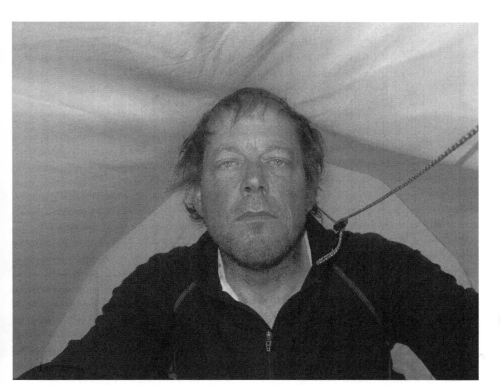

doing LOTOJA, but to be able to have biked to the South Pole makes it worth doing it every day.

Journal — 14 December 2013:

My anniversary. Media has been so good to put up with me and my crazy bike store and even crazier South Pole expedition. I have accused her of not supporting me in the past, but really she has been great at enduring my craziness.

Four days prior, when Daniel had called Media on the satellite phone and told her he probably wouldn't be able to make it to the South Pole, she had given him her full support to continue on. He had feared he was going to be the guy who tried riding to the South Pole with punch, but no follow-through, but Media had given him the support he needed.

Blog—14 December 2013:

Whiteout

I want to dedicate this day to my wife, Media (ma-DEE-ah). She has supported me and put up with me through the bike store and now this crazy expedition.

This morning was cloud covered again but it was still possible to see, so I made good time riding the bike for the first few hours. Then at 11 it started to snow. I could still see but had to slow down to be able to stay on course. I was still able to get about 9 miles during my first 5 hour shift. It was looking like I would have an awesome number of miles by the end of the day.

With the snow everything was white, but I could still make out the route a few feet in front of me. After lunch, however, all contrast was gone and everything was just white. I struggled, weaving back and forth across the hardened trail, and had to constantly get off the bike and search for the trail. This quickly erased all hope of getting a decent number of miles in today. Then just before six it finally got to where I could occasionally see well enough to follow the route, and then the last hour or so it was good biking again. I was able to pull out a 15.2 nautical mile day. Not as good as I had hoped, but better than what it could have been.

Weather for tomorrow is supposed to be about the same with a bit more wind.

The tracks of Fearless John.

Journal — 14 December 2013:

It started out cloudy today but there was still enough contrast to see by. I got a lot of good distance and good speed biking for three hours. Then it started to snow. In order to stay on the resupply road I had to switch to pushing the bike most of the time. The bike is working well on the resupply route, but if I get off of the route the snow is too soft and I can't go very well. Hopefully the snow gets harder by the time the supply route ends at Thiel Mountains. After that I won't have a packed surface. I stopped for lunch with 9 miles. I knew there was a risk that while I was stopped conditions could get worse, but I need the break and food. It was relatively warm, so I put on my parka and didn't bother setting up the tent.

After lunch, it got worse as I had feared. I could no longer see well enough to follow the ski tracks. Oh yeah, at 81° 22' I could see from the tracks in the snow that Juan got on his bike[15]. He rode for a short distance, probably less than 1 mile. Then he went back to his skis.

So after lunch I had a hard time seeing Juan's ski track which was how I was staying on the route. At one point I even went in a circle and was headed the wrong way, but the GPS and compass showed I was off and I got back going right. I would find the route and try and follow Juan's tracks but this new snow was making the tracks fainter and the no contrast lighting made it difficult. I kept pulling out the compass to get me back to the route but for about three hours my progress was very slow. I prayed a lot for help being able to see and to find the packed route. I got help a lot. Then Juan's track was gone from the resupply route. So it got even harder to follow the route. Finally, a little before six, the sun broke through enough that I could see to follow the route. Still, I would lose it frequently, but it kept

---

[15] This was the first time that Juan Menéndez had actually tried riding his bike. By this time, Daniel figured that, even if Juan Menéndez traveled the rest of the way by bike, he really could not count this as a biking expedition. Yet, as time went on and biking conditions continued to improve, the tracks in the snow showed that Juan Menéndez continued to ski and rarely used his bike.

getting better and eventually I was back to riding almost all the time. Juan's ski tracks have not returned to the route yet. I asked when I called in to ALE if Juan was back on the route but I don't think they knew. They said he was having a tough time. They also commented that he will be the first to ski to the pole with the bike on a sled. They also said I am outpacing everyone else, which makes me feel good, but I know things will be hard when I reach the end of the resupply route that helps me so much. I just hope I can get good mileage in now and that when I reach the end of the route I will at least be able to manage to get enough miles to be able to finish in time. Sorry for the sloppy writing, but I'm trying to go fast so I can get to sleep so I will be ready for tomorrow.

I was worried for Juan Menéndez. The reality is that traveling in Antarctica is extremely difficult. The fact that I could not see his tracks meant he was at least a little off track. I knew he had experience in navigation. Yet I was still worried, but hoped that he was making good progress.

Blog—15 December 2013:

3 Days in a Row!

It has now been a month since I left home. It has been quite the adventure so far. It was cloudy again today with more light snow. The snow is getting softer and the contrast was near zero.

All day I could never see where I was going, where the hard snow vs. soft snow was and I had to constantly watch the compass to keep moving the right direction. I only got 7 miles today but I think only about 5.5 in the right direction. I kept having to bring myself back on course. I stopped several times today and waited hoping for better light but it never came. Finally I had enough. I think the cloud cover is supposed to move out soon, but it is sure to be replaced by a good headwind. Nobody said this would be easy.

I hear it is bitter cold back home. Maybe it is warmer here than in much of the USA right now. I really need some nice sunny days to get the snow hard again.

I don't know what is wrong with my inReach. I turn on tracking but it says it has sent 0 of 0 points. It is very frustrating.

Being just a few feet off the packed trail made travel much more difficult. It reminded Daniel of a trip his father took him on when he was a kid.

"My dad learned about a place to go hiking, Brown Duck basin, and got instructions on how to get there. We packed up our packs and got in our station wagon and headed out. When we got to the dirt road that would take us to the trail head it was dark. My dad was told to drive as far up this dirt road as possible and then the trail head would be on the right. The road was really too rough to be driving this station wagon on at all. My dad would have to go as fast as he could down a dip and across water and hope to have enough speed to be able to clear the loose rocks to make it up the other side.

"Eventually we got as far as the car could go and slept for the night. When we got up in the morning there was no sign of a trail head. My dad figured we had gone down the wrong dirt road, so we set out up the old mining road to the top of the mountain. The climb was steep and at places my dad had to take off his belt and use it as a rope to pull Mike and me up the small cliffs. Eventually we got to the top of a ridge and looked down into the valley and saw a little lake. We hiked down to the lake figuring we could fish there and then return to the car.

"When we got there the lake was really more of a mosquito pond than a lake. I don't think it was deep enough to allow fish to survive the winter. We followed the sound of a stream and worked our way back down to the road. We had to jump from bolder to bolder, climb up and over or work our way under fallen trees. Finally we got back to the car, and noticed that a quarter of a mile down the road there were a bunch of cars. My dad had just made it too far up the dirt road in a car that didn't even belong on that kind of a road. So we decided to make it easier to move by leaving our packs at the car and ran out to the lakes to go fishing. We followed that same stream back up to the lakes, only this time we had a trail to follow. It was so easy compared to the route we had taken back to the car even though it was only a few yards away from our previous route.

"After we got to the lakes we fished, and then went back to the car to sleep for the night. The next day we once again hiked out to the lakes and fished and then returned. I was just a pre-teen and in a matter of two days we ended up hiking more than 50 miles, with a large amount of that 50 miles being without a trail to follow. It was an exhausting trip.

"Later when I was in scouts we did a 50 mile hike that took about one week. We started at Mirror Lake and finished at Moon Lake which was the starting place for my earlier trip to Duck Basin. On the scout trip I had brand new shoes from K-Mart. The shoes fell apart after about a day of hiking. It did something bad to my feet and it was so painful to walk. But still that 50 mile hike with the scouts was much easier than the 50 mile two day hike we had done with my dad."

It is amazing that Daniel Burton could, with numb and stiff fingers as well as frozen mind, essentially write his autobiography in his tent out on the ice. It is more than Shackleton ever did, even if Sir Ernest would ever have dared to be so self-revealing. There are all different kinds of courage.

Journal — 15 December 2013:

> Really bad day today. It was cloudy again. The day started with it being nearly impossible to see anything. Again the contrast was near zero so I could not follow the supply route. I try using the compass, but there is nothing to sight off of, so I end up weaving back and forth across the route. I kept hoping eventually the light would get better, but it never did. I unloaded my bags at one point and found my polarized sunglasses hoping it would help. I stepped on the sunglasses on the flight from Punta Arenas to Union Glacier and broke

them, so they just ended up getting lost in the sled bag. I found them and duct taped them together. It kind of worked, but still the contrast was too poor to navigate. The recent snow adds a soft layer and also adds to the no contrast. I spent a lot of time trying polarized glasses, normal sunglasses, my goggles with the facemask, the goggles without the facemask, and no eye protection at all. Nothing worked. I did ride the bike today, but mostly pushed through soft snow. It is warm, not above freezing, but warm enough to make the snow softer. It was just a bad day. I normally quit at eight and sometimes stretch it to 8: 30 or nine. Today, I quit at seven. I just couldn't take it anymore and the clouds are more solid than ever. Hoping tomorrow is better. I think I only progressed about 5 miles south even though I did 7 miles of travel.

Mtbr Forum:

"Because his original plan was to do this supported, I had no interest in following it, but now that he is on his own I'm interested to see how this pans out."

Blog — 16 December 2013:

Do You Know Why They Sing That Song?

S 81°56.649' W 078°57.421' 20 nm today 496 to go.

If every day were like today everyone would bike to the South Pole. Make no mistake, today was once again the hardest day of my life, but 20 miles?... I'll take that!

Finally a sunny day. I could see where I was going and it was up a nice incline with soft snow and large sastrugi. But after that climb, the day had a lot of flatter sections with good snow conditions. I was able to ride up and clear some nice slopes without having to resort to hike-a-bike! It was hard work, but I was able to lay down some serious miles. By the end of the day I was exhausted as always, but kept pushing to be able to hit 20.

I listen to scriptures on Sunday but other than that have pretty much ridden in silence, except for the talking to myself. This afternoon I put on some music. "Du Hast" is a great song to get you through some nasty sastrugi! When I first started listening to the music I started singing along. When there is nobody around for thousands of miles (OK, there are a couple expeditions closer than that) you can sing as loudly and badly as you like and nobody will ask if you know why they sing that song.

A word on the numbers. My Dad was concerned that my mileage was wrong. The thing is, I am not traveling straight south. There are crevasses that have to be avoided. Some of these are known from the history of other expeditions, others from a combination of ground penetrating radar and ice flow rates. Also, sometimes I have to go around sastrugi, and of course sometimes I go a bit extra from errors in navigation. So my miles traveled are not the same as miles made good which is not the same as miles straight to the pole. The only number that really counts is the south part of my coordinates, so I will include my coordinates in future posts. Each nautical mile is 1 minute south assuming you are headed straight south. So if I get 15 miles that gets me about 1/4 of a degree, and of course 90° is the number I have to reach.

Journal—16 December 2013:

S 81° 56.648′ W 079° 57.437′

I did it! I got 20 miles in one day. I should be able to complete my second degree tomorrow. Then it is 30′ to my first cache and the 1/4 way south mark. The first thing I did this morning was to find the resupply route. I had to follow my tracks back until the last point that I was on the route and then follow the resupply route until I was as close to my camp as possible. Then I packed up camp and followed my tracks to the route. It was no wonder I had such a hard time following it in the zero contrast conditions yesterday. The route was so soft and blown over that there were long sections that were not detectable. The day started with a good climb with large sastrugi at the top of the steep part of the climb. Then things got good. I was able to ride for miles without stopping and was able to climb all the way up the steeper inclines without resorting to hike-a-bike.

At 16 miles I came to Juan's camp from last night. Today was a great day for the bike, but he skied the whole thing at least as far as I made it today. If I can get another couple of good days in, I might catch up with him, which may not be a good thing, because following his ski tracks helps a lot. I think they said he was at 87° 7'. That would put him 11 miles ahead of me. I'm not worried about who gets to the pole first because everyone knows he isn't biking.

I may be getting a bit proud. I think about all the things I will do when I finish... telling doubters I told you so, going to outdoor retailers and showing off the bike to all the companies that sponsored

me and showing that I am using their products, thinking about what to say in speeches, etc. Pretty arrogant of me when I am still less

than a fourth of the way there, but I'm feeling like I will make it. I know it will be different after the halfway mark, because there will no longer be a supply route to follow. Hopefully by then the snow will be hard enough to bike on without the resupply route. Also hopefully, I will be able to navigate well enough to get to the endpoint. In the meantime, I need to get to my cache before I run out of fuel.

I think I'm allergic to my sleeping bag. Thinking back I may have been a bit puffed up after sleeping in it at home but didn't realize it. I'm going to sleep with it only covering my legs and leave my pants and socks on so that I reduce contact with the bag and use a blanket and my jacket and parka to keep my upper body warm.

Songs (and skills) my mother taught me.

Blog — 17 December 2013:

You Can't Rollerskate in a Buffalo Herd

15 nm S82°10.500 W079°47.247

I knew as soon as I started this morning that I would have to be happy with whatever I got.

Today was everything I had told people that it would be. Cold, uphill, 20-30mph headwind in the snow. It was definitely the hardest day of my life, again. One of the climbs today was by far steeper than anything I have done since the first couple of days.

I have passed my second degree! So I am now more than 20% of the way there and that is the 20% with the most miles and most climbing. Weather forecast for tomorrow is the same as it was for today, so I guess I have another hard day ahead.

When I was a kid my mom had a record that had a song on it that said you can't roller skate in a buffalo herd. That song kept coming to my mind today.

Journal — 17 December 2013:

15 miles. S 82° 10.501′ W 079° 47.247′ 482 miles to go.

It was windy today, making it very difficult to bike. Also, my legs just didn't want to do the work today. It was a climb all day and sometimes it was pretty steep. I saw tracks in the snow showing that Juan rode his bike yesterday. He went for about 2.5 miles before

going back to skis. I kept thinking of a song my mom had on a record when I was young. It said, 'You can't roller skate in a buffalo herd.' I couldn't help thinking, 'You can't ride a bike wearing skis.' I am trying an experiment tonight. I am sleeping on top of the sleeping bag. Forgoing the air mattress and wearing warm clothes may be easier than inflating and deflating the mattress each day and maybe will keep me warm without the allergy problem.

Blog — 18 December 2013:

Brilliant Plan

S 82°29.707 W 079°28.320 20 nautical miles.

I didn't realize it at the time but that was a brilliant plan. I decided to get to the cache today. I would do 10 miles, set up the tent, eat and make some new water, and then do another 10. What I didn't realize was that while I was eating the wind would stop and the snow would turn hard. I thought it was going to be an extra long day, but I cranked out the last **ten miles in 4 hours**. Now I am at the 1/4 way south point (or close enough). Once again that was the hardest day of my life.

Uh oh. Is Daniel starting to disintegrate?

These are stupid, but when I was working so hard that my eyes were about to pop out of my head they seemed good.

A few thoughts:

- On a spin bike, turn the resistance up as high as you can and still be able to turn over the pedals, I mean even harder than that. Now ride like that for 10 hours a day for two months and you will have an idea what it is like to bike to the South Pole.

- When working that hard, there are no songs that have that slow of a beat, not even elevator songs.

- In Antarctica there is no one to give you the Heimlich.[16]

- You can't bike wearing skis. (You can't roller-skate in a buffalo herd.)

- When you listen to songs in alphabetical order you realize how many duplicates you have.

- No matter how puffy and chipmunk looking you are when you wake up, you still can't store too many sports beans in your cheeks.

- If I had more speed I could have caught some serious air off some of those sastrugi. Just think of a fat bike flying off a four foot drop

---

[16] The night before while eating dinner, a bad case of hiccups attacked Daniel. Trying to eat with the hiccups turned out to be dangerous. Some food got caught in his throat. It was a scary few minutes as he choked on the food with hiccups preventing him from clearing his throat.

with two sleds. I, however, was going quite slow and rolled over the drops.

- Patrick could make some nice jumps out here.

- If a tree falls in the forest and nobody is there to hear it, does it make noise? I would tell you, but there are no trees, let alone a forest.[17]

- When you are dead tired and don't want to go on anymore, it is not a good time for Pink Floyd's *Goodbye Cruel World* to come up on the playlist.

---

[17] Antarctica has to be the quietest place on earth. There is nothing making noise. Even the wind does not make noise, as there is nothing but snow for it to blow against. The only thing that would make noise that he could hear was Daniel himself.

- 2.5 of 150 does not count as biking.[18]

- I'm biking in Antarctica! :-) Meanwhile my family is living in a cold home because we can't afford propane. :-([19]

- Why do I have to make so much yellow snow? OK gross, but the next one is also.[20]

- It is hard to keep your nose clean when there are so many layers on your face. Clearing the nose while biking and not getting it on the layers takes a special technique.

- Where is all that snow coming from, and where is it going? (There is a constant flow of snow drifting in the wind coming from the south and headed north, there is a nearly endless supply of snow, and a nearly endless distance it can drift.)

- Don't cry over spilled rice, it is less weight you have to drag.

Is Daniel losing it? You decide.

Journal — 18 December 2013:

S82° 20.000' (?) W079° 34.225' (?) 10.2

This line is nearly illegible.

Sorry. That was writing with big gloves on.

S82° 20.00' W079° 34.225' 10.2 miles

My cache is at S 82° 29.720' so about 10 miles. I stopped to melt more water and I'm going to go until I get to the cache and then hopefully drag the cache the extra .28 miles and stop at the ¼ way south point. 624-472 = 152 so far. 624÷152 = 4.1 miles per day average so far.

---

[18] This is how far Juan Menéndez had traveled by bike up to this point.

[19] It was hard for Daniel to think about the fact that, due to the solar heating, it was warmer in his tent than it was in his home back in Utah.

[20] Daniel was drinking hot chocolate all day while biking. It tasted good, and help provide needed calories. When he ran out of hot chocolate and had to resort to sports drinks, he realized that drinking hot chocolate made it so you had to make yellow snow every time you stopped. Drinking sports drinks did not have that effect.

You have to wonder. Haters gonna hate?

Mtbr Forum:

However, the reality of the situation so far would indicate it to be a long shot. So far he has averaged between 1 and 1.3 mph, less than 10 miles a day in riding. I can only assume he'll hit some easier riding that will allow him to get higher mileage in. If not, he's on pace for this thing to go for 70 days. If I recall from his earlier blogs, he had hoped to ride close to 40 miles a day?

Journal—18 December 2013:

S 82° 29.707' W 079° 28.308'

It started out windy today. I worked hard and biked and pushed up hills. I realized that if I got 15 miles in, then I would run into the cache at 5 miles into the next day's travel and have to stop and reorganize everything and decided I would rather do that at the end of the day break rather than have an interrupted day of travel. So I decided to stop after 10 miles, melt new water, eat, and then go until I

got to the cache and maybe I would do a shorter day tomorrow. It took me seven hours to get the first 10 miles, but then, while I was taking my lunch break, the wind stopped and the snow drifts turned hard. Add to that some downhill that let me kick it up a gear or two[21] at times and I cranked out the last 10 miles in four hours.

I was drenched by the time I was done, but very happy. Now we will have to see how I travel with all the new weight. I decided to leave the breaking into my cache igloo until the morning so I can get video. The camera was complaining about the battery not being compatible, but I think the problem was just that the camera was too cold. I don't know the temperature, but it is a bit colder than it was when it was cloudy.

Blog — 19 December 2013:

Uphill Battle

82°45.000 W 079°39.270 16 nm

My grandmother would see a beautiful sunset and say it was the most beautiful she had ever seen, and she meant it. So when I say that each day was the hardest of my life, it is in honor of her, because it really is the hardest day of my life every day of this expedition.

I added the food and fuel from the cache to my sleds. It was heavy. Today of course was a lot of climbing, testing my strength against the heavy sleds. A lot of slow cranking on the pedals today. I ended up getting 16 miles but I had to bike past my quitting time to do it. I have to call in my position to ALE every day and so I need to end in time to set up the tent and give them a call. I hope to get up early tomorrow and get back on my schedule that gives me a bit of a buffer if needed to be able to hit my goal.

After learning what my new sled weight was going to be like and seeing that it was a never ending up hill day, I set my goal for the day to be 82°45' south. As you can see I just made it. This makes me 15 arc minutes away from the 83° mark which I should be able to get tomorrow. I believe it also set the world record for the greatest distance

---

[21] This was one of the very few times that I was able to use a gear other than the lowest gear on my bike. I pushed very hard trying to get to the cache before my scheduled call in time.

traveled by bicycle towards the South Pole, which was previously held by Eric Larsen.

They say that a fog is moving in, which means another few days of not being able to see where I am going. Not looking forward to that.

Journal — 19 December 2013 am:

Just retrieved my cache. It was a lot harder to dig out than expected. Now I get the joy of trying to get everything to fit in my sleds and dragging more weight.

Journal — 19 December 2013 pm:

S 82° 45.000′ W 079° 39.270′ 16.1 miles 11 hours.

I started late this morning. I spent the first part of the morning organizing the new stuff into the sleds. The sleds are now a bit heavier. I will eat as much as I can as quickly as possible and always add mix to the drink so I can get rid of that weight. With the extra weight and climbing today it made for a very hard day. I didn't have a lot of energy. I spent a lot yesterday. There were still a lot of good rideable sections. Juan rode for about 1.25 miles along today's route. I need to get rest and start early tomorrow and get what I can in while the weather is good. They say fog will be coming in the next few days. Joy... More days of not being able to see where I'm going.

For situational awareness, refer to Professor Murphy.

Blog — 20 December 2013:

Nothing Ever Goes As Planned

S 83°00.500' W 079°52.769' 16 miles

Overall a nice day today. A lot of climbing and some soft snow. Pretty much like any other day—I crank hard and keep going south.

Today I started making plans in my head, but like Styx says, nothing ever goes as planned. I will reveal one plan tomorrow and the other when I get to 85° south.

I now have my third degree. 85 degrees (half way) is 8 GOOD days' travel ahead. They say clouds headed this way, which means more of the low contrast days. Not looking forward to that.

Saw my first penguin today. OK, not a real penguin, just a sastrugi that looked like a penguin. When I get back I'll have to add the picture of it to the blog.

Journal — 20 December 2013:

S 83° 00.500' W 079° 52.769' 16.5 miles 3559 feet elevation.

Today was a relatively easy day. I should've pushed harder and gotten 20 miles, but I just didn't have the willpower, so I did a lot of thinking and planning today. First I started to think of all the things I can leave at the halfway point. I think I can reduce the weight by at least as much as all my food weighs. The first 30 miles was very hard. My sleds were just too heavy. It is all about being light enough, having enough float that you don't break the top surface of the snow. So I am going to go ultra weight weenie and get rid of every ounce I can and then hopefully with two sleds I can keep them from breaking the top crust. The last half has a lot of climbing but not quite as steep as the first. Those first few days I had to put all my weight into the handlebars just to be able to move. It was extremely difficult and

slow. In order to make it to the Pole I need it to be easier than those first days.

Mtbr Forum:

Daniel Burton seems to be holding his own so far, all things considered. Eric Larsen wasn't making big miles at the beginning of his bike attempt last year, either, which is why he pulled the plug after 10 or 11 days. As long as Burton banked some time and planned for supplies, sheer stubbornness may allow him to pull it off. Will he end up pushing his bike most of that distance? Hard to say. Maybe.

Journal — 12 December 2013:

S 83° 07.155′ W 080° 3.086′ 7.5 miles.

I suffered my first mechanical breakdown at about 5 miles into today's ride. The free hub quit working so that the rear wheel could not turn without it pushing the chain and pedals. I took the hub apart and the pawls in the hub, or actually the freehub body where the pawls fit in, was broken. There are a lot of pawls in this hub so I got rid of the ones where the freehub body was broken. It works now, but the spring tension on the remaining pawls is low so they don't spring out as well as they should. I am guessing I will be riding with no free wheel action before the expedition is completed.

It was now apparent what the popping sound was that Daniel had sometimes heard when he would start pedaling. It was the sound of the pawls slipping and then catching. The guy on MTBR was wrong. Daniel was pedaling most of the distance and only pushing when he had to. The extremely heavy work load caused by biking uphill into a head wind, dragging two sleds through the snow, was much greater than what the freehub was designed to take and it was now starting to break into pieces.

Blog — 21 December 2013:

A Day of Rest

S 83°07.155' W 080°03.086 7.5 miles

Lunch break

I suffered my first mechanical breakdown today. At 5 miles into today's ride the free hub quit working, which means the wheel could not spin without the pedals turning, or no coasting. I never coast on this expedition, so not a big deal there, but it can result in the chain getting all messed up, and it helps to be able to position the pedals before starting. So I stopped, put on my parka and took the rear hub apart. The free hub was broken where one of the sets of pawls fits in. I took that set of pawls out. It now works but the other pawls don't spring out as well as they should since one set is missing.

I am a member of The Church of Jesus Christ of Latter-day Saints or as most people know us, Mormon. One of the things I have struggled with since I decided to do this expedition is what to do about Sunday. I have always liked to make it a day of rest. On the first Sunday I tried to just put in an easy effort, but that just isn't possible, and it got super windy so I quit early. Last Sunday again I thought I would try and make it an easy effort, but it was a zero contrast day, and ended up being very difficult.

The plan: I am stopping now, fixing a meal, and then I will do a second session of 5 hours. Then tonight I will put in an extra session of biking, and take tomorrow, Sunday, off as a rest day. Then I will get up early Monday morning and get an extra biking session in. Hopefully I can still get 3/4 of a degree of progress in today and Monday.

Blog – 22 December 2013:

Fixie to the South Pole

S 83°22.564' W080°03.774 total miles for Saturday 24

The weather forecast for today said it would be cloudy, but it is a beautiful sunny day with a little wind. I am going to spend the day sleeping, using the solar panels to recharge stuff, eating, and just taking a nice day of rest. After going so hard every day for so many days I was really looking forward to this day off, and now that it is here it is great to relax for once.

I got within about .25 miles of Juan last night. I really didn't want to pass him so I stopped a little earlier than planned and set up my tent. I think I am far enough from him that he probably won't even know I am here, and of course he will be traveling today so I will be a day behind him when I start tomorrow. I am not really worried about Juan because he isn't biking[22] to the South Pole anyway. He rode another 3.5 miles yesterday, but still has done less than 10 miles by bike so far, and the rest of the distance has all been by ski.

We will see how it goes, but I am hoping that I will be at 85° and half way south by next Sunday and then I can use that as a rest day to get ready for the last half. My freehub is broken, so I am essentially riding a fixie the rest of the way. It is a bit of a pain, because starting in snow is already a bit of a challenge. Then add pulling sleds, and then the fact that I need to roll to the right spot to get the pedals in the right position to start nice and smooth. It makes the start more challenging. I didn't think I really needed brakes, but they help with getting started. Also it isn't a true fixie because I can still shift gears, which I did a bit yesterday as there was a bit of a downhill.

Blog – 23 December 2013:

White and Blue

---

[22] Daniel Burton's 6th great grandfather, the famous Daniel Boone, was a great tracker, having been able to read the tracks left in the ground. But Daniel Burton did not need the skills of Daniel Boone to read the record left in the snow. There was no mistaking ski tracks as bike tracks.

S 83°46.000 W 080°06.042 16 nm, 24 for the day

239 down 385 to go.

There is no morning or evening or night—just day. So this "evening" I'm having breakfast food. Some oatmeal with apple cinnamon and some scrambled eggs with bacon. However, the egg breakfasts are only 1.5 servings in size so I add some of the breakfast mix in with it.

I keep wondering when I will see the Thiel Mountains. All I have seen for a long, long time is a sea of white and most days some blue sky. I thought today, the only reason I keep going is it always looks like there is a cliff just a little way off in the distance, and when I get there I'll throw everything off it.

Daniel recalls, "It was a strange feeling out in the middle of Antarctica. Every direction I looked it was the same, a few feet of ice and snow and then what looked like the end of the world."

But really, even though it is insanely hard and at times I just would like to quit, I feel like I'm going to make it and I can endure another month of this. If I can keep averaging 1/4 degree per day then I have about 25 more good days and I should be there.

The wind picked up today which helps. It makes it harder to keep frostbite away, but it also helps dry me out some. The conditions right now are probably the best for biking I'll get on this expedition, which means I can now travel for miles without getting stuck in soft snow, but it is always a lot of work to move forward so I sweat a lot, which of course is dangerous. It is a balancing act of adjusting gear to stay warm but not too warm.

Journal — 23 December 2013:

S 83° 46.000' W 080° something

24 miles today. It was a hard day. I started real early to make up for yesterday's rest day and got my 8 miles in early, so I stopped at 8 miles, set up my tent and took a nap. The problem was I was soaked from working so hard. I tried to lay everything out so it could dry and get in my sleeping bag, but I was very cold and I couldn't sleep well and everything was still wet when it was time to go, so I ended up leaving late. Then I had to do the last 9.5 hours without taking a break. The snow and road are as good as I can expect so I can basically ride for as long as I have strength, but I get so sweaty I have to stop and push to dry out. I have to make sure to push the bike the last mile to get a little dried out before I camp.

Juan traveled 5 miles yesterday by bike and what I saw of his travel today he did 2.25 miles. I seem a bit occupied with how many miles he is biking but when there is very little else to see I can't help it. The only thing I see is white snow in all directions and today a blue sky. If not for my gear it would be a two color world. The mountains are coming soon. That will give me something to see on the horizon.

Daniel recalls, "With the conditions so good for biking, I was surprised that Juan Menéndez would continue to ski. As noted in this journal entry, he biked 7.25 miles total and skied probably another 28 miles in those two days."

Blog — 24 December 2013:

All I Want For Christmas

S 84°01.000' W 080°08.372' 16 nm

Very windy and cold today. I added my Pearl Izumi barrier jacket and pants to my normal layers. Days like today are so hard to get that right balance of frostbite protection and warmth but not too warm. I struggle with my hands a lot. I have to add and remove layers of gloves often to get things right. I've found though that the ice buildup on my face mask makes a good wind block.

At times today I was turning the pedals so slowly that I was constantly on the edge of not being able to balance. The wind was straight on, no need for a compass to navigate, just head straight into the blowing snow. At about half way through the day I decided to try and make my setup more aero. So I shortened the ropes to the sleds so the first could draft off of the bike, and the second sled could draft off of the first. Then I took the panniers off the rack and stuck them in the sleds. I think it helped. The panniers create a lot of drag in the high winds.

Merry Christmas everyone. I love Christmas. I am one that thinks Christmas songs should be listened to as soon as it starts snowing. I have never been away from home for Christmas before. So what do I want for Christmas? The strength to be able to go 16 miles tomorrow and each day.

A few years ago my daughter promised that if she could set up the Christmas tree she would take it down after Christmas. She never did and the tree stayed up in the front room all year. I am hoping that the tree will still be up when I get home and then I can have a big Christmas party.

I love Christmas trees. I have a few of them decorating my bike store. During the holiday season I decorate them as Christmas trees. I remove the decorations after Christmas, and when anyone asks why I have Christmas trees set up during the non-holiday season I claim that they are pine trees and not Christmas trees.

Journal — 24 December 2013:

S 84° 01.000' W 080° 08.372' 16 NM

Christmas eve, alone in a world of white. It is hard to be away for Christmas. I left before Thanksgiving so the real Christmas season started after I left. Even though there is snow everywhere it doesn't feel like Christmas here.

It was windy and windy and windy today. There was also a lot of climbing and large sastrugi to deal with. A very miserable day. I kept saying I don't want to do this anymore and I can't wait to go home, but I would remind myself that this is what I signed up for and I can endure another month of this, and if I quit now it would end up with me having a world record that would maybe last until next year, but if I finish I have a world first that can never be taken away. I know, vain, but I need it to be able to use it to pay off the loan for the expedition.

When I called home tonight they told me that Borealis and ALE are working to get a new wheel to me. It will be interesting because the current wheel is glued to the tire. At the tire pressure I am running I could get tire creep on the rim which could cause the valve stem to get ripped out giving me a flat. We will see how it goes. It is late and I need to sleep so I can call Carissa tomorrow and then have a hard Christmas day biking south.

Although Daniel's family was in another hemisphere, thousands of miles away, he felt they were always close to him. His wife and four children were in his heart. His youngest son, Myron, who was planning to leave for his LDS mission to Barcelona, Spain, in August 2014, asked him for his Borealis bicycle as his "inheritance." Burton still doesn't know what to think about Myron asking him for his inheritance *before* he left for Antarctica. Daniel's oldest daughter, Carissa, was serving an LDS mission in Croatia during the expedition. His oldest son, Stephan, was in Michigan with his wife, Tina, finishing his Ph.D. His daughter, Danae, was a social worker, working with children during the epic ride. Daniel's wife, Media, a high school math teacher, kept the family together as he rode.

Oh, one more thing. I have prayed a lot for strength to be able to endure. Today the wind was so hard I kept trying to put plastic bags around my gloves to keep my fingers safe but the wind kept blowing them away and then I had the chain drop between the gears and the spokes and get stuck. I was very frustrated and prayed that I could endure and be patient and if possible to have less wind. It did calm down to where I could finish the day riding. And now that I'm in my tent it is back to very, very windy. I have to say that my prayer was answered.

Blog — 25 December 2013:

Merry Christmas

S 84°09.000 W 80°12.595 8.4 nm

Just like the weather forecast said, it was very windy this morning. So I decided to sit out the early morning and sleep, then do my two sessions of biking in the afternoon and evening. I did pretty good for my first eight miles, but cranking that slow and hard makes my back sore. I will eat some dinner and then get the rest of my 16 mile quota I have set for myself. If I can do that each day I'll be at the half way point this weekend.

I hear a rumor that a sponsor is sending me a gift. Kind of seems like something out of *The Hunger Games*. Anyway I'll tell you more when it gets here.

I hope everyone is having a great Christmas. I got to call my daughter who is on a mission in Croatia. It was great to be able to hear her voice. I really am grateful to the SatPhoneStore for making that possible from the most remote place in the world and of course making it possible to update the blog each day.

Journal — 25 December 2013:

S 84° 15.000' W 080° [illegible] 14.6 miles

Christmas! It was the worst Christmas of my life, alone, windy, cold, and alone. I did get to call Carissa on her mission in Croatia and I called home twice but it was still hard and an emotional day for me. I slept in this morning because I knew the weather called for less wind in the evening. So I did 5.5 hours and got 8.4 miles and then ate and did 3.5 hours more and got 6.2 miles which is pretty good. I still don't see any mountains ahead... Nothing but white. I am so ready to be done at this point, but I'm not even halfway there. It seems like forever ago that I started and seems like it goes on with the same empty horizon forever but I think I can keep a ¼° a day pace going which is 23 more good days of travel and I figure I can endure that. But honestly, I am not too excited about the same hard work for the next month. But when it is all over I think I will feel like it was worth doing and it is too late to back out now. All my life I have thought what if this is all some big thing where everything is just put on for me to see. I guess I don't know how to describe it but they made a movie, The Truman Show, which is exactly like what I had always thought. Egocentric I know but still a thought I had. Anyway I now hear of all these people following my expedition and in a way I have turned my life into The Truman Show only not in the same way that I had always imagined could be what is real. Anyway, strange thoughts.

Daniel flashes back. There he is, Truman under the dome. "At this point I am thinking, what have I done to myself? I now have a following of people that is anxiously waiting for the latest news. When I had battery issues and it took an extra day to upload a blog entry, my wife would get people calling her all worried that I had died, or something really tragic had happened. I had really turned my life into the Truman Show."

Daniel the Explorer Finds His Groove

Truman's dilemma. Like René Descartes, Daniel had long contemplated the idea that life might... *MIGHT* simply be a figment of his own imagination. Perhaps it was a scene in a production for which he had not auditioned and where he could not find his way "off stage" into reality—a place where he could not peer through the "fourth wall" to see who might be the audience out there, comfortable in their own reality. Now that "dream state" feeling was totally creeping him out.

The explorer is, by definition, an existentialist. Once you are in the uninhabited outer space or inner space or the featureless, comfortless limbo of the poles, literally the "ends of the earth," some place where people are not supposed to go, you are all alone in the ultimate quiet, the ultimate solitude. Are you really there? Are you really doing this? Prove it. Out there, Daniel mused, "maybe everyone else is just a projection. The only one I can prove exists is me." *RIMEO ERGO SUM.* I explore; therefore I am.

But then, people came to Daniel's rescue by simply showing up. If a person walks out of the Antarctic ice gloom and into your little bubble of "cold" reality and gives you duct tape to fix your Antarctic sled, then that person (and his duct tape) has to be real, right? Perhaps not, perhaps just the results of a vivid imagination.

Journal—27 December 2013 11 pm:

S 84°49.000' W 080° 35.750' 16.8 nm

Today was a bad day. It started good when the ALE snowcat, pulling three sleds, stopped and gave me some duct tape. I thought the path left by the sleds would be great and maybe I could reach 85°. The path was good but the lighting was bad and my legs just didn't want to go but I went anyway leaving late at 10 AM. I decided to get some video and while I was doing that my quick release on the rear wheel broke and I lost the sled hitch and jammed my chain between the gears and spokes. After fixing that and moving the sled rope to the seat post, the rear hub quit working and I would get a lot of slipping. So I took the spare derailleur cable I had and weaved it around the spokes and the cassette (the gears). Then the chain wanted to jump down a gear so I adjusted the shifting. At this point I was just tired and wished I was approaching the finish instead of halfway and started pushing the bike. After a little while I got back

on the bike and into expedition mode and started eating sports beans every mile. It helped a lot. I was climbing a bit, but with a short day was able to get my 16 miles. Tomorrow I should reach ½ way. I am already more than ½ the total miles.

Mtbr Forum:

I didn't say he wouldn't make it. I just think lack of preparation and a terrible setup—2 sleds!—is going to make it...hard, but sounds like he is learning as he goes. I'm rooting for him.

But, of course, the person in the telephone is real. Back in Eagle Mountain, Media got a call from her husband. He was on his satellite phone in his tent in Antarctica informing her that his solar panel could now be used because the sun came out and so he could recharge his computer. However, he cautioned, he could not blog to his expedition followers until the computer's wi-fi was back in action and it was important to keep the blog entries going out. Daniel asked Media to handle this one and she jumped at the chance to notify the blog audience.

Blog—28 December 2013 posted by Media Burton for Daniel:

HALF WAY!!!! But Wi-Fi Batteries not charged

Sorry about not having posts the past few days. Daniel called from (Antarctica) and said that it has been cloudy and his wi-fi connection equipment has not been able to get charged.

He said that he saw the arctic truck driving out on the ice. He arrived at 84.33.423 on Thursday the 26th, and 84.49.000, traveling 16 miles, on Friday the 27th. He called a few minutes ago to say that he has now passed 85 degrees, or the halfway point. His cache is still five miles away. He is hoping to charge batteries on Sunday so that he can resume his posts.

Thank you to all who are being so helpful and supportive. This wouldn't be possible without you.

Arctic trucks and snowcats...angels? Or demons?

Later, referring to the base camp at Union Glacier, Daniel came back up on the air and blogged retroactively,

December 26, 2013—And Then It Went Downhill

South 84 ° 33.423 West 080 ° 25.032 18.8 miles

There was an elevation profile of the route in the dinner tent at base camp. It shows that at some point there is a good downhill. I was starting to wonder if I had already hit it and it just wasn't as big as I expected. But shortly after starting this morning I hit the downhill. It was great to get a break from all the climbing. Of course, I now have to climb it again, but it was a nice relief. Adding the last night and early morning miles in, I was thinking I might get a 30 mile day. Then I saw the first person that I have seen in what seems like forever—or at least an arm. An Arctic Truck was headed back from its trip to the pole. The driver waved as they flew past. After the truck went by a fog moved in and I lost the ability to see anything. The easiest way to navigate was to follow the new path from the truck, but it had pulverized all the snow, making for bad biking conditions. Also, there was a bit of wind and it got really cold. I started adding layers to my body and hands but I just couldn't keep my fingers warm. I'm not going to let frostbite end my expedition, and I had all the miles I needed to get. So I ended early and failed to get the last five miles that I needed to get thirty. Oh well, twenty-five on the records worked and I had now traveled over 300 miles, which is the record for the most miles traveled by bike in Antarctica.[23] It also means I can reach the halfway point on Saturday.

Lesson learned: The tracks left by the Arctic Truck that was headed from the South Pole to Union Glacier made things much more difficult. What had been a somewhat packed route from other expeditions was turned into a soft and bumpy mess. Biking in the truck's tracks was terrible and for the most part worse than biking on virgin snow.

Blog—27 December 2013:

Don't Spill the Beans

S84° 49.000 W 080° 35.750 16.8 nautical miles 9 hours 4,390 ft.

I started the day tired and not wanting to ride. I recorded some video but just didn't have the strength to work like I should. It was cloudy and low contrast, making it hard to see. So while the snow conditions were great, I just wasn't doing well and I had my worst crash so far. When I started, I had a bunch of honey stinger waffles and sport beans. They were heavy so I ate them as fast as I could. I ran out of waffles yesterday. If you don't seal your ziplock sandwich bags, you will spill your beans. They ended up being a gooey mess in the bottom of my pannier, but I had eaten the rest of them, so I gathered the sticky, gross beans and put them in a bag. The rest of the day, I ate a handful of beans every mile. That might sound like a lot, but I was biking at 2-3 knots. After I started doing that, my energy returned and I finished out the day getting my target minimum of 16 miles. Tomorrow should be a short day as I will reach 85 degrees after about 12 miles. I will then take a rest day on Sunday, and get ready for the last half.

Surfing the sastrugi

Imagine slaloming down a ski slope...on a bicycle. Imagine surfing the big rollers on Oahu's North Shore, only the waves are carved from ice and you do this...on a bicycle...with your eyes closed. Daniel had cycled over anything he could find in Utah including a frozen lake and he had held his breath over crevasses and snow hills in Antarctica, so now he plunged down sastrugi, often during zero visibility whiteout conditions.

---

[23] Eric Larsen had set the record for the most miles traveled by bike the year before when he biked 1/4 of the way and then biked back to Patriot Hills. Now, Daniel had broken Eric's record.

Biking through sastrugi in a whiteout was very difficult and dangerous. The crash that Daniel refers to here is an example of that. While biking over a sastrugi, the ice dropped off sharply on his left. Daniel fell into the drop off. While lying at the bottom of the sastrugi, Daniel realized that a broken bone or a broken bike could end his expedition, so he committed to himself that he would stop and get off his bike when riding over sastrugi in whiteout conditions. This, however, was not a commitment he was able to keep, since frequently he did not realize he was on a dangerous sastrugi until he was in the middle of it.

Journal — 28 December 2013:

> Thiel Corner S 85° 04.981' W 080° 46.897' 16.5 to 17 miles 4428 feet
>
> I thought that Thiel Corner was at 85°. It is almost 5 miles more than that so I thought I was going to have a short day because I was planning on stopping at the cache and then taking Sunday as a day of rest and sorting out what goes back to Union Glacier, what goes to the Pole by plane and what I take with me. It is great that it is 5 miles more than planned because I then got a full day of travel in today. Sometimes things work better than planned.

Mtbr Forum:

> I wouldn't compare anything Mike C [Curiak…the Cyclists' Hall of Fame setter of the standard of expeditionary legitimacy] did to Daniel's trip. Mike C prepared thoroughly both physically and mentally.

Daniel has been fortunate enough to be in some good news stories, and unfortunate enough to have been on the inside of some really ugly news stories. He learned that it is impossible to really understand what is going on from the stories on the news, in the papers, and on the web. Unfortunately, this forum poster made a judgment without knowing the details. Daniel trained well physically, mentally, and emotionally for the trip, and as the challenges of Antarctica presented themselves, Daniel's training allowed him to succeed where more seasoned explorers, whom the forum poster and Curiak would approve of, had failed.

Journal:

> I think I came close to getting snow blind yesterday. I rode all day with no eye protection. Even this morning and a bit tonight my eyes were giving me problems. I got my hands so cold that they hurt when I got them warm again. It is the first time I've had that problem on the expedition. I'm so worried about frostbite that I don't

even let things get that cold. Today's ride seemed like it was mostly uphill, yet the GPS doesn't show that. I'm more than halfway and I am almost at half the final altitude. I think I have done all the bigger down hills. So I've climbed more than half of what my gross climbing will be.

Track of the cat.

I was following the track left by the snowcat yesterday but for some reason the snowcat weaved back and forth worse than a drunken sailor. It was filled with new soft snow drifts because it was windy today. Finally, I started using an old track that went straight. It was easier to ride because it was already hardened by the sun, but wasn't so old that it had bad snow drifts, and for some reason it didn't have many new snow drifts. At 85° I called home and told them I was halfway. Then I continued on to the cache. When I got here, there were black flags all over and I didn't know which cache was mine. I called Union Glacier to try and get help but then I found it. The name had just faded on my flag. It was nice knowing I don't have to wake up early and get moving.

Daniel explains, "The snowcat showed up at the halfway point while I was camping there. I talked to the driver of the snowcat and asked him why he weaved around so much. He said it was because of the whiteout. He could not see where he was going and had to rely on his GPS which would show that he was a few hundred feet off one direction. Then he would correct and end up a few hundred feet off the other direction. When it used the same route I was using, the snowcat was both a blessing and a curse. It often created a packed trail that made travel easier, but frequently it left an indentation in the ice that would be filled in with soft snow. At times it was easier to just ride to one side or the other of the tracks left by the snowcat, but even then the tracks would cross back and forth across my route."

Blog—28 December 2013:

Ultra Weight Weenie

South 85° 04.979 West 080° 46.905 Elevation 4,434 16.5 miles

In some ways, you could look at this expedition as a three part journey. The first part was the climb up from the coast of Hercules Inlet. It was the steepest part and hopefully the softest snow, and very

difficult. The second would be from near Patriot Hills to Thiel Mountain, which is what I have just completed. It was still very hard, but they have driven machines from Patriot Hills to here so there has been a packed trail to follow. This should have been the best biking conditions of the journey.

The third and final section starts now. From here on, there is no more packed route and there is a lot of climbing. Hopefully, the snow is harder now than it was during the first section. But other than that it will be a lot like the first section. The weight of the sleds killed me on those first days. Trying to pull all that weight up those slopes was just too much. If the next section goes as bad as the first I will never make it. So here is the plan: I'm going ultra weight weenie. I'm going to get rid of my brakes, my big chain ring, water bottle cages, racks and panniers. I will tape over the bolt holes for the cages and the racks so I don't get snow and extra weight in the bike and I'm getting rid of the bolts. There is a lot of gear I brought that I just don't need. I brought a bunch of charging wires and electronic stuff that I'm not taking the rest of the way. I think there is more weight in the gear I will drop than what I'm picking up in my resupply so I should be the lightest I've been up to this point. By going as light as possible I think I can still get the 16 miles per day and complete the expedition.

Daniel realized, "The weight of the equipment and bike parts that I took off here was minor compared to the weight of the food I left behind. I took a bit of a gamble here. I calculated how long I thought it would take to get to my next cache and left behind all the food I figured I didn't need so that it could be flown back to the base camp at Union Glacier by the Twin Otter when it stopped to refuel. The gamble worked out well as I arrived at the next cache quicker than I calculated."

Audio books in Antarctica anyone?

In the middle of all this, Daniel was studying German, and some days as he traveled, the Book of Mormon in German played on a continual loop through his headphones. Burton laughed as he reflected back and said, "I think I have the Book of Mormon memorized in German." In addition to his Deutsch scriptures, he also had audio versions of the English Book of Mormon and Bible playing in his ears as he huffed and puffed and pedaled. He listened to the iPod to break the silent void that was Antarctica and to draw inspiration to keep going. The scriptures were a great influence but at times he needed music. He would use the upbeat music to get him to push harder, but also he would use the music as a way to track time and distance without looking at the GPS. Eight songs would take less than one hour and result in a little more than one nautical mile of travel.

Blog—29 December 2013:

Weight Loss Among Giants

S85° 04.979 W080° 46.90.5 Elevation 4,434 feet above sea level.

I am making good time, but the sastrugi are getting bigger and more challenging especially since I have the gears wired to the spokes which means I cannot stop pedaling as I ride through the sastrugi. When I get whiteout and sastrugi at the same time it becomes very tricky as I am basically biking blind through rough sastrugi. Also, at the half way point I had sent back anything I figured was extra weight that I did not need. This included the brakes from my bike. I am able to manage without the brakes, but it makes it tricky to bike through the sastrugi.

Brakes are a luxury?

Daniel makes a technical judgment. Cyclists, what would you have done? "Shimano donated the components for my bike, but they only had hydraulic disc brakes, not mechanical disc brakes. I didn't want to worry about the hydraulic fluid freezing, so I found some old and heavy Shimano mechanical disc brakes. I decided that the advantage that the brakes gave me was not worth the weight of the brakes, so I got rid of them. Looking back, this was a good choice, and if I were doing the expedition again I would go brakeless the whole distance. There is little room for luxuries in Antarctica and the brakes were a luxury."

Blog — 29 December 2013:

Weight Loss

S85° 04.979 W080° 46.905 Elevation 4,434 0 miles

I spent the day sleeping and repacking all my gear. The bike has been stripped down as light as possible and I left all my extra food and gear to be taken by ALE back to base camp. I don't know how much my new load weighs, but I think I left behind more weight than what I have moving forward. My goal is to get 1/4 of a degree each day. This would give me 20 days of travel and 3 rest days, getting me to the South Pole by around the 20th of January.

Daniel recalls now. "Wow, what an accurate prediction. There were days that I was able to get more miles than I would have guessed would be possible, but then the last few days were much more difficult than what I expected when I wrote this."

Excuse me, sir, but I believe you dropped your mitten.

Journal — 29 December 2013:

No travel today. I took a lot of food and stuff I didn't need and gave it to the guys from ALE. They are here working on leveling the runway and unloading fuel. The planes that fly to the South Pole cannot go the full distance without refueling. So they land here and refuel and then continue on to the South Pole. They also found my mitten that I lost a couple of weeks ago clear back by the Patriot Hills. It will be nice to have two mittens.

Reading his journal, Daniel shakes his head, "It is amazing that I could have dropped a mitten in the middle of Antarctica, and have someone find it and return it to me. The sad thing is a day or two later I lost it again. :-(I had several layers of gloves that I would wear. I had a pair of thin thermal Pearl iZumi gloves. I then had some nice down filled Canada Goose expedition gloves that I would put on over the top of the thermal gloves, and then I would put the down filled mittens over the top of the down filled gloves. This would work great, but I was working so hard that I would sweat a lot and after a few hours my gloves would get wet and then freeze. If I were to do this again I would take three pairs of thermal gloves, three pairs of down gloves, and three pairs of down mittens. Then when one set would get wet and cold, I could swap it out for the next set."

Journal:

I don't know how many miles I can do moving forward. I am hoping for 18 with 13.5 hour days but usually it turns out I can't do as much

as I think I can. I want to at least get ¼ of a degree each day so that I can finish before the season ends.

My battery situation is not good. I can't seem to get the phones to take much of a charge. I've gotten rid of the Sherpa [a battery pack I used to charge equipment] because it says it has a bad battery and so I can't use it to charge anything. So a lot of other electronics also got sent back since I can't charge them.

Daniel feels the presence of the other expeditions.

Journal—30 December 2013:

S 85°24.242′ W 081° [something] 20 miles

Overall, today was a bad day. It started fine. It was sunny and low winds. As I was getting ready to go, a guy walked up to talk to me. His expedition had arrived at Thiel Corner along with another expedition while I was sleeping. He was driving an Arctic Truck supporting a lady that rode a three wheeled trike to the South Pole [Maria Leijerstam]. Her original plan was to do a real expedition and carry all of her gear herself, and the truck would stay in sight but out of contact. The driver of the truck told me that it didn't work and that she had to take all her gear off of the trike and put it in the truck. Then she was able to travel well, but the three wheels making three paths in the snow would not work in soft snow. The trike worked because they were on the US maintained road that was well packed. Anywhere any snow was drifted on the road she would have to use her hands on the wheels to turn them, giving her "three wheel drive." He told me several times that Maria had it easy, but I don't think anything in Antarctica is easy. They had just driven from the pole to where I was camping and so they had seen what I was about to go through. Maria's expedition was easy compared to doing a real expedition, but it was not easy. He warned me that ahead there was a lot of soft snow, and LARGE sastrugi.

Notice that Dan is doing well and Dan is writing well. The pen is mightier than the sword, but the head is in charge of the pen.

"I then started south. To my surprise there was a nice snowcat trail to follow. I was doing well following it when the snowcat passed me on its

way back. It had picked up the people from the ALE van that must've broken down. The fresh tracks from the snowcat were not as good as they were before it made the return trip, yet still I was able to get 10 miles in less than five hours. *And that is where things went bad."*

Thiel Mountain breakdown. The kid can fix it.

Just when Dan was in a groove and, emotionally at least, everything was "downhill," *the bike stops here.*

Journal:

> The freehub went out in the rear hub/wheel a long time ago. I wired the cassette [the set of gears on the rear wheel] to the spokes and have gotten a lot of miles that way. However, it made it so I constantly had to adjust the shifting. Then today after 10 miles the cassette ended up being crooked and I could no longer adjust the shifting to keep the chain in one gear. I had to push the bike the rest of the day. It turned cloudy and contrast dropped but I continued on. At 17 miles, I found where they picked up the van. It was a mess of ruts and piles of snow. After getting through that I was tired and wanted to quit but I continued until my normal 8 PM quit time.

Daniel reminisces about his youth as a mechanical kid who could take something apart and put it back together until it was fixed. "When I was a kid, I took everything apart. A couple of years ago I was talking to my dad about this and he said that I would never get them put back together, and I told him, 'No, you just don't realize how many things I took apart and did get back together.' I think this helped me be a problem solver, a troubleshooter. I find a way to take something apart, put it together, repair it and make it work." Out here, Daniel was not a performer in "Antarctic Survivor." This was not a reality show on ice. This was a real wilderness survivor proving the feasibility of crossing a polar environment on a mountain bike modified into a snow bike.

Journaling on:

> I then set up the tent and took the wheel inside. It took a lot of work to unwire the cassette and I found I had broken one spoke. After I got the cassette free I opened up the hub and it was a mess of broken parts. There is no way to get it to be workable. So I am walking until the new wheel arrives. It is supposed to be in Punta

Arenas on the first. Then they have to fly down. I don't know how long until I get it. In the meantime I will just walk.

Daniel glumly recalls. "I was very discouraged at this point. I really did not want to have to push my bike all the way to the next cache. And then later that same day…"

Journal—31 December 2013 am:

> I decided to give the wheel another try. When I put the wheel together it seems the cassette goes in the right place and is centered. I used tie wire and did my best to make a more sturdy wire job. I said a prayer asking for help. I know God can make it work if he wants. The question is, is that what he wants for me? I hope so.

With the fear coming back, Daniel mutters, "This really was the most desperate I would feel during my whole expedition. The headwinds were harder than I could have possibly imagined. I would get so tired of the wind, and I would pray that I could just get a little break from the wind. No wind, however, meant a whiteout, and I hated the whiteouts. They were so frustrating. I would struggle with my goggles fogging up, I would try using sunglasses, and then a different pair of sunglasses, and then a different pair of goggles. Nothing I did worked. I knew it was a big mistake to go without eye protection but sometimes that was the only way I could continue moving forward. In an interview, Vesa said that whiteouts were the thing he hated most. I'm not sure which was worse, the whiteouts or the wind, but neither of them was as bad as the thought that I would have to push my bike across the frozen wilderness. After putting it together, I was sure that it would not work."

Journal—31 December 2013 pm:

> It worked! I was careful about not pushing too hard so I wouldn't break it again, but the wheel worked. After a few hours I noticed it was a bit spongy at the start of peddling. That was the first thing to happen with the old setup, so I pushed the bike the rest of the day so I would be able to make it work at least some miles each day until I get the new wheel.

During the climb from sea level to over 9,000 feet, Daniel realized that he wasn't alone. Even though he could see no one and could hear no one, Daniel Burton kept a prayer in his heart—and his mind. He said he was constantly "biking and praying with God."

Blog — 30 December 2013:

Ups and Downs

S85° 24.242' W081° 07.397' Elevation 4,422 ft. 20 nautical miles

The day started out sunny with low wind. I was able to crank out a quick 10 miles. The Thiel Mountains are visible to the west. It is nice to be able to see something besides just a sea of white. The afternoon turned cloudy and the visibility dropped. I was able to get a very nice 20 miles in for the day. It was a day of going slightly up and down with the altitude flirting with 4,500 ft. I can't tell if what is ahead is a cloud bank or a steep climb. If it is a climb, that is fine as the pole is still 5,000 feet higher than I am now. Hoping to get at least 16 miles tomorrow.

Blog — 31 December 2013:

It Was A Hill

S85°42.000' W81° 24.400' 18.2 nautical miles Elevation 4,969 ft

It wasn't a cloud bank.

When I woke up this morning I had this strange feeling that I was camping in a forest alongside a little trail. Of course there is no forest here.

This was a very real feeling for Daniel. Slipping ever deeper into that dream state alienated trance, he thought,

Had I unzipped the tent and looked out on a beautiful forest with birds in the trees, a little brook full of fish, and a nice trail through the woods I would not have been surprised. But of course, there were no sounds of trees blowing in the wind, no birds chirping, no babble of a brook, and outside my tent was nothing but a frozen sea of white.

Lots of clouds today and low visibility. The day started with a little downhill and then a big climb to 4,800 ft. The rest of the day was up and down, ending near my home elevation of 5,000 ft.

There have been several Arctic Trucks and ALE vans returning from the South Pole to Union Glacier, returning polar travelers back to base camp in preparation for the end of the season and the coming of winter. They left big ruts in the snow. I followed in the tracks but it made for some wild and crazy riding. It was like riding very narrow, technical, single track while being blind. However, when I could manage it, I was able to make good time.

Journal—31 December 2013:

The trucks that have returned from the South Pole look like they had a hard time with the soft snow. They left really crazy ruts. I was able to follow in the ruts and bike pretty well but when the slope got too steep or the ruts too crazy I would get off and push so that I don't ruin the wheel again. I got 18.2 miles, which puts me at S 85° 42.000'. If I can get 18' tomorrow I will reach 86°. Somehow saying six down and four to go makes it sound like I am getting close. The first time I did the Canyonlands White Rim 100 mile mountain bike ride in a single day, when I got to 80 miles I got this great feeling that I would be able to complete the hundred miles. I am thinking I will feel the same when I reach 88° and have 8° out of 10° done.

It was weird but when I woke this morning I felt like I was camping in a forest by a path. No forest, but I was able to see the Thiel Mountains to the west most of the day. I really wished I was about done today. I am so ready for this to be over. But then I decided to enjoy it while I am here because when I am done there will be no going back. I spent some of my time today taking pictures of the mountains and bike etc. Still, I'll be glad to be done with the expedition and go home. I have decided when I get to the base camp the first thing I will do is go get one of the big chocolate bars and eat the whole thing. I guess I will also need to go take a shower. I am sure I stink real bad.

Daniel smiles, "I did stink really bad. At times it was bad enough that it was hard to be with myself…in a sleeping bag…in a tent…or riding the bike."

Blog – 1 January 2014:

Pick Your Poison

S86° 00.000' W081° 35.300' 18.5 nautical miles Elevation 5,356 ft

6 down, 4 to go! (Degrees, that is)

A wind came in and blew out the clouds, making a nice sunny day. However, the wind also filled the deep ruts from the trucks with nice soft snow. Outside the truck tracks, the snow was just on the edge of being too soft for biking. So should I ride inside the ruts, or outside?
The sleds felt heavy and it seemed most of the day was climbing. I spent a lot of time slowly cranking up the hills. I really wanted to get to 86 degrees, but it didn't look like it would happen. Then the sun did its magic to the snow, making it harder, and the slope leveled off. I had to work really hard to get to 86 degrees. I got it just in time to set up camp.

I have to make sure to quit on time. Otherwise, I don't get enough sleep and it makes for a hard day the next day.

Journal — 1 January 2014:

New Year's Day

This is one of the few days I get off at the store. Of course I didn't get to take a holiday today. I passed Juan's camp at 17 miles into yesterday's ride and 13 miles into today's ride. I get closer and closer to him. Then I take my Sunday off and he pulls back ahead another day. But it doesn't matter because he will not be able to say he biked to the Pole. He has probably gone less than 20 miles[24] by bike so far.

I could tell this morning that the clouds were gone because of the heat of the sun coming through the tent. There was also some wind. It filled the truck ruts with soft drifts of snow, making the insides of the ruts real bumpy and very hard to ride or push through but still they were usually better than going outside the ruts. There was also a lot of climbing. So far my rear wheel job is holding but I worry about putting too much force into it. So if the hill is too steep or the snow too soft I get off and push. I didn't put a lot of food in my bag because I was planning on getting the cache and new wheel at 86° 30'. But the next flight to Union Glacier is on the fourth [of January] which is when I planned on getting to the cache. I put what I figured was 10 days of food plus a bit which should last until the eighth [of January]. Hopefully they can get the wheel and put it in a cache before then.

S 86° 0.000' W 081° 34.300' 5325 feet 18.5 miles in 12 hours. 251 miles to go which is 14 days at 18 miles a day.

Adding in Sundays, it would mean getting to the South Pole on the 17th. I think I can do another 16 days. I was looking back in the Journal for when I got my first degree. Didn't see it but read where I figured I would never make it. A lot's changed since then.

---

[24] I was keeping a rough mental tally of how many miles Juan Menéndez was riding his bike. Sometimes it seemed like a silly thing to be doing, but spending all day every day alone means I had to do something to keep my mind busy. Adding up Juan's miles and seeing how far behind him I was made for some good mental activities.

Really, Dan? Speaking of funhouse pictures, take a look at yourself.

Blog—2 January 2014:

This Used To Be A Funhouse

S86° 18.765' W081° 37.745' 19 nm, 232 to go, Elevation 5,772 ft.

24 hrs of low wind and no clouds has allowed the sun to hit the snow from a full 360 degrees, which makes for great snow to bike on. The climbing continued today. John [a friend that trained for LOTOJA with me and that I wanted to include in spirit on my expedition] would not like this. It's like that road coming back from Elberta.[25] The road seems to go on forever with a constant climb. However, here in Antarctica, this does go on forever, or at least for hundreds of miles.

---

[25] Wikipedia says that Elberta, Utah has 236 people living on 13.6 square miles. The town center is an abandoned wooden Sinclair gas station from the 1940s and a post office in a nice corrugated metal hut. There is terrific cycling all around; just bring your own water bottle and energy food. In the winter, this is good training for cross country bicycling in Antarctica.

As I go up in elevation, the air gets colder and thinner. They say that in Antarctica, the physiological effects of the altitude are like being 2,000 feet higher. So far, however, the altitude has not been a problem for me.

I think I'm gaining ground on the other expeditions. Juan's ski tracks ahead of me are now only half a day old. It seems I've been gaining 3 or 4 miles a day on him. However, on Sunday I will take a rest day which will give him the chance to get another day ahead.

I have started a routine of taking a break every mile, which turns out to be about how long it takes me to listen to all the different versions of Pink's *Funhouse* that are on my iPod. These breaks allow me to get a drink and return the circulation to my hands and feet. I pull a lot on the handlebars, which means that I probably need to lower the stem. But I'm not going to risk loosening and tightening those bolts in this cold.

Thinking about that, Daniel notes, "One of my major goals was to return with all ten fingers and ten toes. I have had frost bite on my toes from winter campouts in Utah. Now I had to work real hard to keep my fingers and toes from freezing. Anyone that has spent much time outside in the cold knows what it is like to get your hands too cold, and then the extreme pain as they regain circulation. Because I was working so hard to avoid frostbite I only had this problem a couple of times. I was able to arrive at the South Pole without getting frostbite on my fingers and toes; however, I did damage them. To this day my toes and fingertips are all numb. I hope someday they will return to normal."

Journal—2 January 2014:

S 86° 18.765′ W 081°37.745′ 19 miles in 10 hours. 5772 feet.

I had a hard time convincing myself to get up and going this morning. It will be nice to sleep in on Sunday. It looks like I will get to 86.5° one day earlier than I had planned. I had planned on that being where my next cache would be but we are waiting for the wheel before they place the cache. Not much wind means not much new drifted snow and lots of sun means nice hard conditions.

And then Daniel made a mistake.

The chagrin comes back when Daniel remembers. "At the halfway point I had reduced my food supply to what I thought I would need to get to 86.5°, knowing that I had a lot of food in the last cache. I figured that getting the cache early instead of the originally planned 87.5° would allow me to better spread out the food. However, I was getting more mileage than planned and the wheel was taking longer than planned, which meant that the last cache would end up at the originally planned 87.5°. There would be a really serious danger in getting to the next cache that I did not foresee."

He Did It

The Great Race

Back at Thiel corner, the half way point Daniel had written,

> I spent the day sleeping and repacking all my gear. The bike has been stripped down as light as possible and I left all my extra food and gear to be taken by ALE back to base camp. I don't know how much my new load weighs, but I think I left behind more weight than what I have moving forward. My goal is to get 1/4 of a degree each day. This would give me 20 days of travel and three rest days, getting me to the South Pole by around the 20th of January.

Daniel Burton was, after all, a long distance cycling racer.

So he was competitive and a risk taker. Approaching his last cache with his food running out was a risk and an opportunity. He could go fast and long every day and pass Juan Menéndez. "Again, here I was allowing myself to be concerned with beating Juan. I knew Juan was skiing and not biking so I knew that I shouldn't care if I got there before he did, but I had this internal fear that he would arrive first, traveling almost exclusively by ski, and then claim to be the first to bike to the South Pole. I had pedaled my bike for hundreds of miles following Juan's ski tracks. I knew it was bikeable and wondered why Juan wasn't even trying to use his bike."

Mtbr Forum:

> Juan has also updated a blog, in Spanish. Juan Menéndez Granados - BBC Mundo - Temas. Sounds like he's having a tough go as well, and hasn't yet been able to ride his bike.

Daniel reported in his Journal,

> When I started today, Juan was 8 miles ahead of me. He rode his bike for the last 4.5 miles of what I rode today. I guess I can see tomorrow how much further he goes by bike.
>
> The Thiel Mountains kept getting smaller and further away and finally at the end of the day they disappeared. Now it is back to a sea of white with nothing else. Today it seemed like rolling waves of the sea with each wave being higher than the one before. I was thinking about how at the end if I am not too far behind Juan I could leave

the sleds behind, ride through the night while Juan is asleep, arrive at the Pole, claim victory, then go back and get my sleds. Vain ideas, but it doesn't matter because he isn't going to end up with as many miles as Helen reports she did.

Juan Menéndez and Helen Skelton both used skis and bikes to get to the South Pole. Juan's final biking mileage is not known and so it is hard to say who biked more, Juan or Helen. Based on Daniel's mental tally, Juan had biked 20 miles during the first half (375 miles) of the expedition. After the half way point, Juan would occasionally bike up to one third of the distance he would travel in a day. Many days he did not use his bike at all, and Juan admitted that he didn't use his bike the last week so that he could travel faster. So if you are extremely generous and give him about one third of the final 300 miles, then that would give him at most 120 miles. Helen biked 103 miles.

Blog—3 January 2014:

Enjoy Where You Are

S86° 31.338 W081° 40.189 13 nm Elev. 6,066 ft (220 miles to go)

The snow is hard, the slope isn't too steep, and I got started on time. It looked like it would be a good day. Then my repair job failed and I had to take a few hours to redo it. I should be getting a new wheel soon. With a short day, I got a respectable number of miles. Since I didn't work too hard today, I'm going to make up the lost hours tomorrow.

I'm so ready to be done with this expedition. Time only goes forward, so I am taking the time to enjoy the trip. We only get to live each day once, so enjoy where you are.

Overall, though, things are good. I was planning on being at 86.5 by the end of Saturday, but I'm there now, so I'm already ahead of schedule. I haven't been working as hard as I did those first couple of weeks. I think it is time to pick up the pace. I'll work hard tomorrow and

151

then take my rest day on Sunday. If conditions continue like they are, it should work.

Was Juan Menéndez getting information from Daniel's blog relayed back to him? After Daniel wrote this blog entry, Juan Menéndez started putting in more miles each day. It seemed Juan Menéndez was bound and determined not to allow Daniel to pass him.

Blog—4 January 2014:

This Is Not My Idea Of Fun

S86° 52.546′ W081° 43.409′ Elevation 6,644 ft. 23 nm

I set up my tent yesterday and ate dinner and in the couple of hours that it took me to eat and call in my blog, it went from being a nice sunny day to being really cloudy with no visibility.

I wanted to get to 87 degrees today, so I started very early. But I couldn't see where I was going. The sastrugi are now getting really big and spectacular. But when you bike over them and can't see, it's very scary and treacherous. You'll be going along and all of a sudden you'll have a four foot drop that you didn't even see coming, which is very painful, even if you don't crash. So I was creeping along very slowly for most of the day.

(Mental) foggy mountain breakdown...again.

Finally I got cold and needed to add some layers, so I stopped and ate lunch and added the layers. While I was eating, the visibility improved some, so I was able to travel better. Later on, the sun came out and it got a lot clearer. I could now see the six foot sastrugi that I'd been trying to work my way through before. It was much easier and a lot more fun to be able to pick your way through them instead of blindly hitting them. That lasted about an hour and then visibility dropped to zero again. So overall, I put in a lot of hours but didn't get many miles.

Daniel was experiencing the revolution of rising expectations. "It is funny that I said I didn't get very many miles. Yes, I worked long and hard, but 23 nautical miles is a great number."

Daniel was beginning to break down. His numb hand scrawled disintegrating sentences with a shaking pencil...not very electronic for a computer programmer.

Journal — 4 January 2014:

86°31.338' W 081°40.189' 13 nm 6066 feet.

I got up on time and was on my bike by 8:30. It was sunny—not much wind and the snow was good. I got in a quick 3 miles and then all the wires from my cassette to the spokes broke. I was very sad and started pushing the bike at 6 miles. I realized I had wire in the hood of my jacket and my parka and wire in the window of the tent, so I took all those wires and fixed the wheel again. I think it may hold out this time. Also my new wheel should be placed with my cache in three days so it looks good to go on. I'm only about 7 miles behind Juan. I was thinking today that if I go hard maybe I can get 30 miles a day which would have me finish next Saturday so I'm going to try it. This will of course make it so I pass Juan. It is about midnight and I plan to be moving by 1 AM so I will pass him while he sleeps. I hope that I can then put down enough miles on the rest of the day so that he doesn't catch up with me while I rest on Sunday and then on Monday leave him way behind. It will be cool if it works but like I

said before the main idea of this plan is to get finished with this expedition and go home.

Losing it.

I had miscalculated where Juan was. Not only was I not ever able to get 30 miles in one day, but he was further ahead. So passing him just would not end up happening.

Journal—4 January 2014:

> 86° 52.543 W 081° 43.409 23 miles 6672 feet 198 miles to go

> I didn't take weather into account for my plan. I took a short rest last night and started at about 1 AM. Somehow in the couple of hours I was in the tent it went from sunny to heavy clouds which means no contrast. I started out on the bike. One of the trucks that came back from the pole left a dirty trail most of the time. The darkness of that

dirt[26] helped me stay on track. But eventually I couldn't see it and ended up pushing the bike trying to stay on course and not hurt myself when I would go off 4 foot drops that I didn't see. It was no fun. I expected to pass Juan early but it was almost as if he knew my plan and it seems he biked and skied extra yesterday and today. When I called in they said I was 1 mile behind him. Tomorrow he should get another 15 miles or so. I'll try and get 30 on Monday. I got some pictures of the bike in the sastrugi today. Hopefully it will be useful.

Blog—5 January 2014:

Just Like LoToJa

S86° 52.546 W081° 43.409 Elevation 6,644 ft. 0 nm

It is 198 nautical miles to the south pole, which is 227 statute miles. LoToJa is 206 miles, so now it's just like LoToJa—well, a few things are different.

Wikipedia says that "...the LoToJa Bicycle Classic is a 206-mile (332 km), one-day amateur bicycle road race from Logan, UT to Jackson Hole, WY, USA...LoToJa is one of the longest one-day road cycling races in the U.S, and is the longest one-day race sanctioned by USA Cycling... In 2011, (the race) had over 1,500 riders.

"LoToJa... "LOE-to-juh" by some and "la-TOE-juh" by others...starts ...in Logan, Utah and heads north into southeastern Idaho and winds across western Wyoming. The finish line is near the base of the Grand Tetons at Jackson Hole Mountain Resort (at Teton Village), one of America's top ski destinations. Along the scenic 206-mile (332 km) course are three mountain passes, plus hilly to rolling terrain that results in nearly 10,000 feet (3,000 metres) of vertical climbing.

"...LoToJa is a major fund-raiser for the Huntsman Cancer Foundation, Autism Spectrum Disorder Connections and other medical research foundations. To date, LoToJa sponsors and riders have raised over US$750,000 for these causes.

---

[26] I never could figure out what it was. The truck ended up breaking down and having to be hauled out by a snowcat. It could have been burning oil or something else and leaving a dark mark on the snow.

"...It is estimated the average LoToJa rider will burn up to 15,000 calories on race day and take approximately 11 hours to complete the event."

Daniel went on with the comparison.

This is 21 miles longer. LoToJa is on a road; this is on snow. In LoToJa, I have skinny, smooth tires. Here, I have 5 inch wide knobby tires. LoToJa goes through three states, and, of course, this is Antarctica. It is 100 degrees colder here. LoToJa has three big climbs, but also three nice downhills. This doesn't have as steep of climbs, but you can't coast on the downhills. I travel about 20 miles an hour doing LoToJa, but here I'm happy to get two knots [about 2.3 mph].

LoToJa is a one day event, but I still have two weeks of travel left here. On LoToJa, there are rest stops where family or friends are there to give you food. Here, I drag my food and gear behind me on two sleds. LoToJa has a wheel car that gives you a new wheel if you need it. But here, my wheel had to be flown in by plane. (Huge Thank You to Borealis!!!!! It will be in my next cache). For LoToJa, you have to finish before dark. Well, here I have to finish before dark, too.

So, other than these minor details, this is just like LoToJa. If I can finish LoToJa six times, I think I can do this. South Pole here I come!

Journal—5 January 2014:

Rest day

I slept, ate, and daydreamed about all the different things I can do to get done early. I should make it in two weeks at the most assuming 16 miles a day. But I would like to finish by Saturday. It would require about 35 miles a day which is very ambitious. No matter how it works out though, I think I should make it to the South Pole. They are putting my wheel in the cache and placing it tomorrow. I told him to put it at 87° 30′ but it will depend a bit on where they can land.

Cache #3 S 87° 79.553′ W 081° 42.673[27]

I wonder if I can get close and give them a call and see where it is and if I have an awesome day of travel tomorrow then maybe I can get it tomorrow evening. We will see. I still haven't done a 30 mile day but I hope to be able to do it.

"It is funny how optimistic I could be. 35 miles a day?… in my dreams. Oh, I guess I did say I was daydreaming."

Wishful thinking, but he didn't know that he would have to risk his life to get the next cache.

Blog—6 January 2014:

Crevasses and Sastrugi

S87° 12.000 W081° 47.980 21 nm Elev. 7,425 ft

I finished my 7th degree—only 3 more to go!

Daniel says, "Wow, reading that now brings a huge smile to my face! Especially since I know how many miles it takes to complete one degree of longitude."

---

[27] Here, Daniel had jotted down the coordinates of his next cache right in the middle of his journal entry.

I had a hard time convincing myself to get going this morning. It was windy and cold and I kept hoping the wind would die down a bit. Eventually I decided I'd better get going if I wanted to get a good day of miles in.

Daniel remembered that, "On the second day of the expedition I decided to switch up my daily schedule to try and bike when conditions were most favorable. And I would do that throughout the expedition. This is an example of that. Sometimes my attempts to modify the schedule worked out OK; other times it worked out perfectly!"

Journal—6 January 2014:

The sastrugi are getting really big, which makes for some very technical biking. The sastrugi are sharp, hard, and have 6 foot drops in them. A lot of times there is just enough drop and then rise that it will stop the front wheel, making it very likely to do an endo [biking term for going over your handlebars]. Fortunately, I was always able to get my feet down and stop before any serious crashes. I removed the brakes back at the halfway point. Maybe it wasn't a good idea. Dropping off sastrugi without brakes is scary!

Daniel says, "Yeah, but looking back it was worth it." Tip responds, "Dan, you crazy kid you! Where did you think you were?… in a half pipe in a skaters' park?" This was Antarctica! Was Daniel losing it there at the end?

Around the crevasses and through the sastrugi to cache number three we go.

Blog:

The day was mostly spent climbing. There was one short, steep downhill, followed by what seemed like a wall. I climbed 400 feet in a short distance. Throughout this climb, there were small lines in the snow that, when I first saw them, I thought were crevasses. It turns out that they were. I found a couple that had openings in them. Most of them were about 2 to 5 inches wide, so not enough to be dangerous. But still, I was glad to get off of that slope, both because of the climb and the fear of the crevasses.

Tomorrow's route takes a jog to the west to get around a dangerous crevasse area. The South Pole is only about 2,000 feet higher than I am now, and the climbing should mellow out soon. I should be there at the pole in less than two weeks.

Daniel notes, "It is funny that I was glad to get past the climb. In this area the climbs were some of the easier places to bike. The slope of the hill would make it so the noon day sun would hit the slope at a better angle which would make the slopes very icy. The fat tires had no trouble getting traction on the ice, and the hard ice was much easier to ride on than soft snow. At times while climbing these icy slopes I would weave my way back and forth across the slope to reduce the steepness. It worked well, but it also meant I was traveling along parallel to the crevasses instead of perpendicular which was a bit scary."

Journal — 6 January 2014:

6 Jan 2013

Tip says, "Come on, Dan. Stay with it, boy. That's supposed to be 2014." Ah, but Daniel responds, "I would think that writing 2013 was funny, but it is normal for me to have a hard time switching to the new year. Even in the middle of July I can find myself having to take time to remember what year it is. Worse than that, I often have a hard time remembering how old I am and, when asked, have to calculate it."

S 87° 12.000 W 081° 47.980 2 nm 7425 feet

I am giving up on the 30 miles a day plan and just facing the fact that I will be going into next week before I can finish.

Daniel's stream of semi-consciousness is coming out in a rush.

There was a lot of climbing today, and a lot of big sastrugi. The sastrupi [It should be sastrugi but Daniel's handwriting is falling apart here.] were very dangerous to bike through but I was trying to get my miles so I biked most of them. Several times I got real scared when I found myself in a situation where crash was imminent. Fortunately I always managed to get my feet down in time. I found myself wishing the bike had brakes, but I took them off at Thiel Corner to save weight.

One of the climbs today was very steep and riddled with small crevasses. There was also one spot that looked like it had a crevasse large enough to fall into. I saw it at the last moment and pushed fast to get past it. I just got my cache location and was told there are two crevasses about 1 mile south of the cache and that I should go more west to avoid them. I won't get there tomorrow so I will find out more when I come in tomorrow. I guess this is the scary part.

Broken wheel keep on turning; Proud Daniel keep on burning.

At about 6 pm today I broke a spoke in the rear wheel. That is two spokes now that are broken. With the gears wired to the spokes it puts a lot of strange force on the spokes so it isn't surprising that they are breaking. I pushed the bike about 1 mile after breaking the spoke because I didn't want the wheel to go so bad that I won't be able to push the bike. I will try riding towards the end of the day tomorrow when I know the new wheel is close. I want to be able to say I rode every day so I need to make the wheel last another 17–18 miles.

Russian Roulette or Pink Floyd [hit?] The Wall. Now for the really scary part…

Blog—7 January 2014:

Russian Roulette

S87 ° 28.065 W083 ° 04.102 17.8 nm Elevation 7,803 ft

My final cache is about 4 miles southeast of here. Before I started the expedition, we looked at the ground penetrating radar. The planned route veers a bit to the west here to avoid a dangerous crevasse field that's to the east. There are two crevasses one mile south of my cache, so now the trick is to get to the cache but avoid the crevasses. Once I get the cache, I will come back to this location to get ready for the last quarter of the expedition. From here, the South Pole is about ten days away. I will get some food and rest and then go get the cache in the morning. So tomorrow will be a short travel day and I will have more weight.

Today has been a good day for travel. I was lazy and got a late start, but I knew I would have to stop after about 18 miles so I could get my cache, so I wasn't too worried about starting late.

The climbing continued today. I am now only about 1,500 ft lower in elevation than the South Pole. The sastrugi keep getting bigger and harder to bike through. I manage most of them, but occasionally I have to get off and push to make it safely through them. At one point my bag fell out of one of my sleds, and it took a while before I realized it and I

Picking up my last cache

had to go back and get it. You'd think that I would notice the difference of losing half of my load.

One of the songs that I have on my iPod is *Russian Roulette* by Rihanna. That song played today and it made me think that with all of the crevasses around me that I'm kind of in a Russian roulette game. I hope I can make it to the Pole without falling into one of them. If not, then I guess this will be my last blog post, and I will leave my family at home destitute, trying to repay the loans I've taken out to finance this expedition.

Thank you to the many people who have helped and are still helping and supporting me in this adventure. It wouldn't be possible without you all.

Daniel thinks about it all now. "OK maybe I was playing it up a little, but then again, the danger was real. To this day I have a really hard time listening to the *Russian Roulette* song. The emotional effects of that day will probably haunt me the rest of my life.

"There I was biking through some huge sastrugi. At one point I was next to a big sastrugi and then I turned and looked back and saw that I had just crossed over a snow bridge. In this area there were a lot of small crevasses. I couldn't tell if the snow bridge I had crossed was over a crevasse or just a big sastrugi. Either way, the drop was big enough that it could have been deadly and I am glad that the snow bridge had not given out on me."

We all live by a yellow cycle wheel.

Blog—8 January 2014:

I'm In Love

S87 °42.000 W082 °38.936 15 nm, +8.5 to go to get the cache Elev. 8,239 ft.

I love my new yellow wheel! It looks amazingly cool with the red wheel in front and the yellow wheel in back. It works really well with the DHL sticker. You'll have to wait until I get to the South Pole to see it. The new wheel makes things so much easier. I can now attack the climbs up the sastrugi without fear of breaking spokes, and then when they drop off ten feet, I can quit pedaling and move back behind the seat and not have to worry about going over the handlebars.

I really love this bike! Before I left, someone posted on Facebook about how inadequate the fat bike he had at the South Pole was. The Borealis bike is awesome! I find it ironic that the Borealis will be the bike used for the first bike expedition to the South Pole, as borealis means "northern" and the bike has an Alaskan flag with the North Star on it. I have to find the best pressure for the tire again—low enough to be able to move forward in the soft snow, but not too low so that when I hit the sastrugi, it doesn't cause a pinch flat.

The new supplies from the cache have made the sleds heavy again and it makes the hills and even the flat much harder. I am only about 1,100 feet lower than the South Pole now, so at least there isn't much climbing left. I just have to eat a lot at the stops to give me energy and lighten up the sleds. I also found a Christmas card and Christmas treats from ALE in my cache this morning. I think being alone for so long is messing with my emotions. [Yes...alienation...Truman Show] I was overcome with joy at getting those.

I hear that Juan has been worried that I might pass him. I don't understand why he would care. He gets one more day of biking each week, so I doubt I'll pass him. Anyway, no matter who gets there first, he will not be able to honestly say he was the first to bike to the South Pole. He is skiing to the Pole and rides his bike for a few miles every day or so. For example, yesterday he rode three and a half miles. I don't know what his total miles (ski and bike) for the day were, but I know it was more than 15. Riding for an average of 20% of the daily distance and skiing for 80% of the total distance does not qualify for biking to the South Pole. Besides, he disqualified himself as biking to the South Pole when he rode for fewer than 4 miles out of the first 100. So it really doesn't matter if he gets there first.

Meditation on judgment, repentance, and forgiveness:

Daniel later noted, "Some people were not happy with how I attacked Juan with this post. Yeah, I probably shouldn't have. The facts were not favorable for Juan, and I made the mistake of talking about them in my blog."

Daniel had committed himself utterly to the tune of over $100,000 and the risk of his life alone on the ice for 51 excruciating days in order to claim before the arbiters of world records that he was the first to bicycle (riding or pushing) from the perimeter of the continent to the South Pole. His wheels rolled the entire distance. If Daniel has to defend what is rightfully his as the result of all this sacrifice (including family sacrifice), what must he say?

Juan's expedition was a great lesson learned. He went the full route from the periphery to the Pole by human power, alone. He should have claimed that. He should not have imagined it was something more.

Juan Menéndez would say, "This isn't rideable," so he would put his bike in the sled and ski. Daniel would say, "This is rideable," and he would ride his bike 10 feet and get stuck in soft snow, push his bike another 10 feet and then get on his bike and ride again.

Unlike Maria Leijerstam, the other claimant out there, Daniel didn't have a compacted, marked road. When he could, he picked up ruts, broken trail through the snow, and tracks. No matter how hard his pilgrim's progress sounds, the purist path Daniel followed was in reality much more difficult.

Blog on.

It looks like clouds might be moving in for tomorrow. :(

I'm terrible at biking in the low contrast. But I'm going to just enjoy these remaining days. I can now average about 15 miles and make it to the South Pole by next Saturday. The couple of extra miles per day doesn't make much difference at this point.

Shout out and big thank you to some of my many sponsors, especially Borealis, who shipped me this new wheel, the SatPhoneStore who has provided me with the Iridium 9575 satellite phone so that I am able to make these blog posts, all the guys running my bike shop Epic Biking back home, and all of you who have donated to my expedition. You're the greatest!

Journal:

8 Jan 2013 (!) 87° 42.000' 8100 feet

2013? Daniel is back to trying to bend his frozen hand around the pencil stub and focus his frozen mind.

A very hard day today. Yesterday after riding to the spot on the route that was closest to the cache I set up my tent made my phone call to ALE and to Media and went for my cache. For some reason they put it four miles off the route. It was hard to get to because I had to go through some monster sastrugi and then up to the top of a hill that was near large crevasses. The ground penetrating radar showed that as a very dangerous area. I was seriously worried that that may be the day I die [Bye bye, Miss American Pie]. But I made it to the cache and back. It was an 8.5 mile trip and took five to six hours that would've been better spent going in the right direction. It was great to get the cache and the new wheel. I took it back to the tent and put the new wheel together and on the bike. It was good weather so I took a short nap and headed out. I only got 15 miles towards the pole today, but I am now nine days away if I only get ¼ degree a day and given how things have been going lately and with the new wheel, and most of the climbing done I should get that even in bad weather. Clouds moved in and I think it is zero contrast now so I'm going to get some good sleep and see what I can do tomorrow.

"This cache was placed in a very dangerous place that I was trying to stay far away from. Also, unlike all of the other caches that were right on my route, it was four miles in the wrong direction. Retrieving this cache was the most dangerous part of my expedition. If the cache had been placed along the top of the same ridge it was placed on, but where that ridge intersected the planned route, I would have been safe. I have wondered about the butterfly effect of this also. If I hadn't had to waste half a day to get this cache and then push so hard to make up for the lost time, which caused me to seriously bonk [run out of energy], then I would have been a day or two further along when the last whiteout hit. I would have finished a couple of days earlier and I would not have run out of food. But on the bright side, it added a lot of things that are fun to talk about now that it is over.

"At 87 degrees 50 minutes south I got another bad whiteout day and in the whiteout I developed an idea for a charity. After that, the sastrugi got very small and then no more sastrugi. I followed some truck tracks but they were going east of my planned route. I figured the tracks were still going to the South Pole but maybe the GPS in the truck was just calculating the route differently. When I called in to ALE they told me not to follow the tracks because they may not go to the pole. I then used my GPS to calculate a new route to the South Pole and headed south.

Daniel reflects in a Journal entry,

It turned out that the driver of the truck was looking at the map on the GPS. Maps on the GPS get really funky as you approach the South Pole, and what looked like a short cut on the map was in reality a button short cut.

Daniel coins a new phrase: The Button Short-cut:

Button, button. Who's got the button?

Daniel's father tells the story: "In 1966 we lived in an apartment complex (Ballaine Lakes) just west of College, Alaska. Because of a very wet and boggy spot next to the apartments, the dirt road from the University made a small loop just before turning into the apartment parking lot.

"On satellite images you can see the old road as a scar in the forest. The road went west, turned north toward Ballaine Lakes and then turned west again just before the apartment complex. The road now doesn't follow the same route and is paved.

"One of our neighbors, Dr. Don Button, worked with me at the Institute of Marine Science. Don had purchased a brand new Land-Rover

when he accepted the job in Alaska and was anxious to see just how well it would work in the Alaskan Wilderness.

"To really appreciate what happens next, it helps to understand that the apartments were built in the arboreal birch forest and with considerable boggy areas and permafrost. Also, the loop next to the apartment was only 30 or so yards longer than what it would have been if the road went straight. The reason for the loop was to avoid a very wet bog with permafrost underneath.

"One day on the way home from the University, Don decided to take a short cut and drive straight through to the apartments rather than taking the loop. About 15 yards into the 'short cut', Don's Land-Rover sank into the bog. Using the four-wheeled drive only stirred the thixotropic bog and made it even more liquid. The Land-Rover was hopelessly stuck! It ended up taking several days to get his truck through the short cut. Going the longer way would have taken a few minutes.

"After that, any time anyone took a short cut thinking to save time, but in reality it took longer, we'd call it the 'Button Short-Cut.'"

Daniel explains his Button short-cut:

"The first 25 miles of the expedition, I was able to follow ski tracks left from other expeditions. Then I used the Patriot Hills as a landmark to navigate until I hit the resupply route where I could follow tracks. After the end of the resupply route I was able to follow more tracks left behind by a few trucks that had driven to the South Pole. I followed those tracks until they had taken me several miles off course to the east. I again turned south, but there were no more tracks to follow and no landmarks to help me navigate. So at that point I was completely on my own to navigate to the South Pole. Then there was another whiteout day. All of the previous whiteout days were very frustrating for me because it made it hard to follow the truck tracks, but now that I was on my own, and beyond the dangerous sastrugi, I actually had fun in the whiteout. I tried several different ways of navigating using my compass and GPS. After a while, the fun wore off and I settled into just using the GPS and worked my way south.

"For a couple of days before I left the truck tracks and the rest of the way to the pole the snow was soft. I'm not sure how much of this was because of a snow storm and how much of it was just that the snow does not harden up much near the pole. This meant I was going a lot slower than I was a few days before."

Blog—9 January 2014:

I Bike Alone

S 87° 53.000 W 82° 01.111 12 nm 8,318 ft

Sorry for the low mileage today. My old man eyes just don't do well with the low light conditions like today. One of the songs on my iPod says, 'My shadow's the only one that walks beside me.' Well, I must stink so badly that not even my shadow would bike with me today.

Today was actually the easiest day I've had so far, at least aerobically. But it was a difficult day because of the lighting. The first ten miles were pretty much flat and the sleds seemed to just glide along. Then there was a short downhill. I hit some of the highest speeds that I have gone the whole time, but I couldn't see where I was going. It was like biking downhill with a white paper bag over my head.

I have one fork and one spoon. Usually I can only find one or the other. The last few days it has been the fork. Today I found my spoon so I figured I wouldn't be able to find my fork, but I found it, too!

Journal—10 January 2014, 4 am:

Yesterday was cloudy and I could not see where I was going. I ended up having to push the bike a lot and only got 12 miles in. When I set up my tent to call into ALE and to call in my blog I could see a little blue sky to the east so I thought maybe it would clear for a bit. ALE says it is supposed to be cloudy today. So after eating I looked out and the sun was shining so I got out to get some miles. I hoped to get to 88 before the clouds come back but I just had no strength so I'm stopped again. The sun is shining and I'm going to get some rest but I'm still short of 88.

Daniel realized something. "It was so hard for me to stop here when the weather was great. I wanted to go on, but the effects of going and getting the last cache were too great to overcome."

S88 ° 35.132 W083 ° 13.976 8,866 ft.

Earlier this week, I decided to spend what should have been my sleeping hours to go get my third and final cache. I then put in a full day's ride. The next day I struggled. Then came the white-out day, so I gave up another night's sleep to try to make up for the bad days, which didn't work. This made it so that I had nothing left. I could barely pedal the bike today.

Fear the bonk! Embrace the bonk! Bonk not lest ye be bonked!

What is "bonking?" Bonking is collapsing physically at the height of an extreme physical exertion due to total glycogen depletion. Runners call it "hitting the wall." Cyclists call it "bonking."

Daniel should have seen the bonk coming, but he did not see 'the handwriting on the wall' – or in the journal.

Delorme Forum and "Team Serious": "The last *InReach* reported position I saw was from here ...

It sounds like he may have hit the 'wall' a bit.

Here is to hoping Daniel wakes to fair weather, a slight pushing breeze from the west, firm snow, and a rested mind.

Sincerely, best of luck Dan, your endeavor is a gutsy one."

Blog — 11 January 2014:

Eureka—I Bonked!!

I was reminded of my post about enjoying where you are. I had gotten so focused on finishing quickly so I could go home to my family that I was just pushing too hard. I decided to go back to just enjoying the ride. Today, I took a lot of breaks to eat freeze dried fruits and drink hot chocolate (provided by TheReadyStore.com—Big Thank You!) Pedaling at a bonked effort, I was still able to keep moving and got in a respectable number of miles. I committed myself to just enjoying the final days of what will be the first bike expedition to the South Pole. If it takes a little longer, that is fine.

Blog — 12 January 2014:

Last Week?

Same location as yesterday.

Well, hopefully this is my last week of biking to the South Pole. I hope to arrive by Saturday. Today was a nice sunny day with low winds, but I took a rest day and recharged batteries, both those for my electronics and hopefully my body. I spent the day getting a lot of sleep.

I've been told that Juan is having problems with dizziness and running out of food, so my prayers today have been with him. While our expeditions are different, his being a solo ski/bike expedition with no support or resupplies, and mine being only biking but with three resupplies, we have traveled the same route. I have usually been a day or two behind him, but for the most part we've experienced the same weather and snow conditions. Juan has done a great job and I would like to congratulate him. If I don't finish too far behind him, I may see him at the pole, at base camp, or back in Chile. If so, I'll congratulate him personally. Otherwise, I'll just use this post to say, "Good job, Juan!"

Blog — 13 January 2014:

Master, the Tempest Is Raging

S88° 40.529 W082° 27.680 16nm Elevation 8,961 ft.

Overall it was a relatively flat ride today. If it hadn't been for the soft snow it would have been perfect conditions. With the soft snow, though, it was very hard pedaling. There are now ski tracks from multiple ski expeditions ahead of me. If I follow in their trails, it helps a lot. I am moving at such a slow speed that it is hard to maintain balance and stay on the ski tracks. When I get off the ski tracks I can still go, it is just harder. I am very tired from a hard day's work that didn't result in as many miles as I would have liked.

Daniel Burton's Snow Biking Tips:

If you are having trouble with traction in the soft snow, lower the tire pressure. At times I have had the tire pressure so low that the tube doesn't fully fill the tire. Today I needed low pressure, but not that low. Also, if you come up on a soft patch of snow, move your weight back. With low tire pressure and the weight back, you can power through some pretty soft snow.

Daniel recalls, "The day I wrote this, Juan had tried to ride his bike but didn't make it more than a few yards before switching back to skis. I was able to ride this same section that Juan had to ski. I knew how to ride

in the hard conditions because I biked in the hard conditions and never skied."

When flying back from the South Pole to the base camp at Union Glacier, Daniel shot a video out of the airplane window looking over the route he had just finished riding his bike across and posted it to his blog.

This may not be as interesting to you as it was to me. This short video shows the 'landscape' of the Antarctic ice cap. I didn't realize how much I would be going up and down over and over. It was frustrating to climb a couple hundred feet only to drop back down, especially since the downhill seldom felt like I was going down.

Journal—14 January 2014 am:

S 88 ° 40. – –

Yesterday was a very hard ride. I only got 16 miles in while biking for 13 hours. The snow was very soft because there has been a bit of snowfall and very little sun to harden it. They say it is supposed to snow more today so it may be a hard day today also. I would really like to get to 88° 58' because in the final degree all human waste must be packed out. I would like to empty the system and hope that I can finish without having to pack any out. I really want to finish by Saturday but it is going to be hard given the snow conditions and altitude.

Blog — 14 January 2014:

Soft Snow and Cookies

S88° 42.833 W082° 29.960 2.5nm Elevation 8,962 ft.

It has been snowing today and there has been heavy cloud cover. The snow is very soft. The biking was extremely difficult and I could not see what I was doing. After a couple of hours I gave up and spent the rest of the day in my tent waiting for better weather. I need to at least be able to see where I am going. They say the clouds should break up tomorrow.

I heard a plane fly over today. Hopefully that was a good sign.

I slept a lot and dreamed of big, soft cookies.

Journal — 14 January 2014:

S 88 °42.833 W082°29.960 8962 feet 2.5 NM

Real bad day. I couldn't see and it was so hard to pull sleds through the soft snow. I tried for three hours and then put up the tent and lay down on my thin mat and rested and hoped for a break in the clouds. It never came, so I got out the warm air mattress and set up for the "night." I'm cold and ready to be done.

Daniel, thinking back, recounted, "This was a very hard day, not physically but mentally. I shouldn't have given up. I guess I was hoping that I could skip out on riding in the whiteout and maybe get better use of my energy, but it ended up just wasting a day that would have been better spent getting a few more miles. Also, I was running low on food, and I consumed a day's worth of food but didn't get any closer to the South Pole."

Blog — 15 January 2014:

Chased By Dogs

S88° 55.555 W82° 43.134 13.5 nautical miles Elevation 9,033 ft.

I had this fear come over me today that I would end up biking over 600 miles and end up failing in the last 100 remaining miles. It was cloudy and I didn't want to get going but knew I had to. The snow is still soft, making biking very difficult. But at least there was enough light to see by.

The clouds made two full circle rainbows around the sun and a halo that went through the middle of the sun and around the sky. It produced a pack of sun dogs that followed me most of the day.

DeLorme Forum—15 January 2014:

Hi folks. I have been following the adventures of Daniel on https:// share.delorme.com/DanielBurton and noticed that the map seemed to stop at a point and his tracking points just move back and forth along the edge of the map in a straight line as he closes in on the South Pole, since one of the advantages of the inReach is the ability to track anywhere on the globe I guess I'm kinda surprised that the map seems to be failing. Any ideas?

Apparently, the community was watching and very interested in the achievement unfolding on their screens. A well meaning forum user who was trying to explain the strange mapping behavior gave the following incorrect explanation:

You're misunderstanding how the inReach works. The map isn't failing. It is faithfully reporting the data being sent to it.

The inReach uses two separate satellite systems for two separate functions. The Iridium satellites are used for text communications which will send GPS information along with the message. The Iridium satellites' orbits are polar to polar so communication should be pretty reliable at his position.

The GPS information is derived from the GPS satellites which are near equatorial orbit. I forget the exact term but they generally orbit a few degrees in an angle off the equator. The closer to either pole you get, the less accurate the triangulation is going to be to gain a good fix of your location, particularly if you don't hold the GPS in the correct direction based on the type of antenna being used; in this case, northward. At such an extreme position as being near the poles when standing still, your position is going to rock back and forth a fair amount of distance because the triangulation to your position is constantly changing based on which GPS satellites are being used.

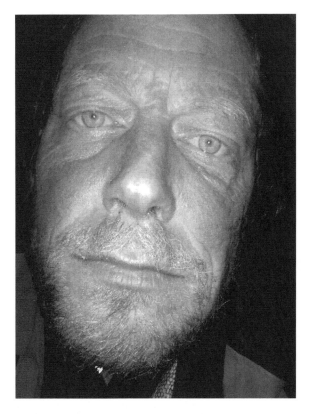

The GPS location the inReach is going to use in the position it sends to the Iridium satellites at such an extreme position will carry this noted error. That's technology for you.

Cheers!

Greg - Team Serious

Dan reflects on Greg's lesson. "Actually, the GPS satellites provide great coverage at the North and South Poles."

Another serious GPS navigator weighed in:

It appears he is using the usual 10 minute track intervals moving at +/- 1.2 mph. It also shows +/- 8,200' elevation. Hover your cursor over a tracking point and left mouse button click should give you the data. Keep in mind that the track connects the points. If he was using a more frequent track interval (You can't with the InReach SE) you would see a more accurate trail. If he was using the PN60w with an InReach, his PN-60 would show a more accurate trail but not on the share.

Team Serious

Another professional analysis provides the correct information:

1) GPS satellites are inclined 55 degrees from the equator, and high enough they generally provide good coverage in polar regions.

2) You can view DanielBurton's coordinates individually by clicking track points. He isn't rolling in a straight line.

The strange behavior on the map is because the cylindrical map projection used by the DeLorme tracking website just doesn't work well in polar regions. In these regions you need to use an azimuthal projection, but azimuthal projections aren't very good for most of the globe where people would be using an inReach satellite tracking system.

3) The projection map on share.delorme.com stops at 87 (north or south) latitude. Anything closer to the pole is drawn against the viewable "edge" of the map; a series of points will show a straight line with approximate longitudes only.

If you want to see what the track really looks like, look at the points in Google Earth.

The only way for the map display to NOT fail that close to the pole would be to use something like gnomonic projector centered on the pole itself.

Daniel explains, "What some people saw here but could not understand with the type of map being used was that I had followed the truck that was taking the Button Short-Cut, then left his track and started going the shortest route to the South Pole. Later, I decided to take a gamble and see if I could find tracks on my planned route. The gamble didn't work out. So I was always headed south, but not straight south. Another thing they don't understand is that you cannot go straight south to the pole. There is a lot of sensitive scientific equipment around the South Pole, and so there is a very precise route you have to take to get to the pole."

Daniel hadn't known that the GPS experts were looking down on him from their Blog Olympus and finding favor with his field expedient methods. Now Daniel was lunging for the finish.

To the nth degree!

Blog — 16 January 2014:

The Final Degree!

S89°09.687 W082°49.224 14.6nm Elevation 9,036 ft

Nine degrees, nine minutes down. 51 minutes to go.

The heavy clouds, low visibility, light snow fall and soft snow conditions continue. Tomorrow's weather forecast is for more of the same. I just have to face the fact that this is probably what I will get the rest of the way.

I have started shouting out the remaining miles as I finish each mile. I don't know why, but it makes me feel good.

Journal — 16 January 2014 am:

S88° 55.555'

Yesterday the snow was soft. It was possible to ride but took a lot of effort. At one point I found the ski tracks from the other expeditions. They are not following in the tracks from the trucks. I tried following them for a while. It is better than out where nobody has traveled but in the end I went back to the truck tracks. They have a firmer base but are a little more rough which makes a bit of resistance for the sleds. Today I have taken a bunch of weight from the sleds and put in my pockets. We'll see if that helps. At 64.445 miles I am probably a good four days of biking left to go. It looks like a bit cloudy today. I'm tired of cloudy days.

The Forum was still there, calculating.

As near as I can gather from the location data provided from the above InReach link, this was the general track of this ride. Looks to me like he has about 75 landlubber miles to go.

Journal — 16 Jan 2014:

S89° 09.687 W82° 49.224

The clouds were bad today and I guess it is relatively humid. I started the day riding the bike, but the soft snow made it real hard and I got so sweaty and it fogged up my goggles. I tried everything but just couldn't keep any of the goggles or sunglasses I have from fogging to where I could see. Eventually the light got so low that I took a chance with snow blindness and went with nothing on the eyes. I also tried making my sleds lighter by putting everything in my coat pockets. It didn't help with the sleds and the weight in the coat was obnoxious so I put stuff back in the sleds. Then when I got to my tent I couldn't find my phones. I had a major panic. If I don't call in each day they will think something is wrong and an emergency rescue would be expensive and put an end to the expedition when I am so close. Eventually I found the phones in a fold of the sled bag. I was so worried that I had left them on the snow a dozen miles back.

Daniel says, "I often have people ask what was the scariest part of the expedition. I think this may have been the most scared I was, or at least the greatest moment of panic. I searched and searched for my phones and couldn't find them. It was a tremendous relief when I did finally find them."

Journal:

I am now shouting out my distance remaining and my # of arc minutes remaining every time I complete another one. I yell about as loud as I can because nobody can hear me. It helps me get through the day and I feel some accomplishment as each mile and each minute are completed.

Journal — 17 January 2014 am:

It is uncomfortably warm in the tent this morning which is a good thing. It means the sun is shining, everything in the tent is drying out and hopefully the snow is getting harder. I am fixing my breakfast and then I will pack and get going. Hopefully it will be a good biking day today. I mixed bacon and eggs into my chicken à la King. A little worried about using two meals, but hopefully I can put the calories to good use today. My feet are starting to get better. A few days ago they were hurting so I took my socks off. I have been being bad and not taking my socks off at night. I wear about six pairs of socks so taking them off and putting them on is a pain. Anyway I took them off and my feet were in bad shape from being wet all the time and biking and walking. And my fingers and my toes are always numb now. I think the fingers are numb from being so cold so much. Biking makes my feet go numb and my toes get cold. 59.4 NM to go.

Daniel says about this journal entry, "I didn't realize it at the time but I had just documented the day I lost the feeling in my fingers and toes.

177

When I wrote this journal entry I thought it was just a short term numbness. I often will make my hands or feet go numb when biking but the feeling returns after a few hours or days. This, however, would be a long term numbing. It is now almost one year since I finished my expedition and my fingers and toes are still numb and not showing signs of improvement."

Blog — 17 January 2014:

I'm Going To Quit ;) —After I've Finished

S89 °19.466 W074 °13.644 13nm Elevation 9,080 ft

Only 46.4 miles to the South Pole, and then I'm going to quit. I am so tired and ready to finish this. Still, at this point, 46.4 miles feels like a long way to go, but I can do it. Today was sunny with low winds. The snow is getting harder, so I'm hoping tomorrow will be sunny with low winds again—I'm hoping, but will deal with whatever tomorrow brings. There's still another good climb between here and the pole.

Daniel explains this post, "I thought I was funny and had been planning this for days. I figured if I posted that I was going to quit it would make people panic, and then when they read the post they would see that I was saying I was going to be able to quit because I was finally done. My wife posted the blog entry for me. Sometimes people that wanted Juan to beat me would post comments to my blog saying bad things about me. And when she posted this blog they posted comments celebrating my apparent defeat. I guess my humor didn't translate to Spanish very well. My wife screened out the comments and changed the title from "I'm Going to Quit" to "I'm Going to Quit ;) — after I finish." When I got home and found out about this, I told her she should have let the comments go through, but by then it was too late and they had been deleted."

Extreme exhaustion doesn't stop Daniel from pedaling...or writing.

Journal — 17 January 2014:

S 89° 19.466 W 074°13.644 13 NM 9080 feet 46.4 miles to go.

I'm trying to figure out my endgame. I have four dinners left and probably enough fuel to cook the meals. If I run out ALE will bail me out but it would be good to be able to finish with what I have. I'm thinking that I will get up in the morning and eat the first meal, then bike 11.6 miles, stop set up the tent take a nap, eat the second meal and repeat until the end. I have been following the trail left by a truck. It is headed more east than what my GPS wants me to do but it is easier to follow its trail than to go out on the fresh snow. If I look at the GPS map it shows the route I should take.

I think the map is strange because it is a Cartesian map and they get weird at the poles, but my remaining miles is dropping well and I'm still west of the designated entry point for the final 3 miles. I figure if I get to 20° west and I'm still too far north I can at that point leave the truck tracks and head to the entry point. I am guessing the hockey stick route the Garmin wants me to take is the shortest route but I think the smashed snow of the truck route is worth what little extra distance I have to travel. However the GPS says my remaining distance is going down faster than it says my miles traveled is going up so maybe this is a good route. Anyway the GPS now says that I am more than 5 miles off route.

It is real cold now. I burned my fingers a couple of times from touching the fuel bottle and touching the stove. The burns happen instantly but go away quickly. I need to be careful.

Daniel reflects, "The fingers were being burned from touching the super cold metal. I had been told that one of the common ways people get frostbite is from working with the stoves. I started being more careful with how I worked with the stove and other metal items and I was able to avoid any problems."

Meanwhile, back at the lab, the Forum says,

As to polar GPS coverage, I note that while I have never been, the polar track geometry is well known. The Constellation is not optimized for polar coverage. With its 55 degree system inclination and a 26,560 km orbital height, the maximum rise above the polar horizon is 14 degrees. There are lots of satellites, and many should be skimming the polar horizon at any given time, some as much as 14 degrees high. A good antenna should pick up enough sats most of the time for a fix. The Helix type antenna (by Inreach) is better than the planar type for wide angle coverage. But odds for a good quick fix is lessened compared to lower latitude locations. I would suggest that if lock up is slow, try canting toward some horizon. The satellites are constantly changing location. While the 55 degrees is not particularly shallow, it was chosen on the expectation that the space shuttle would service the Constellation. This never came to be. The Glonet (sic) Constellation is at 65 degrees and equally high, somewhat better for arctic explorers.

When Dan got to read this, he commented, "Again, funny things people said. The GPS system worked perfectly fine at the South Pole."

Blog — 18 January 2014:

Head Winds

S89° 29.139 W073° 03.322 Elevation 9,160 ft 11 nm

Only 35.4 statute miles left to go

It has gotten extremely cold the last couple of days. I have to be very careful when I get in the tent and unpack my sleds. Everything is so cold that if I touch things with my hands I get instant frostbite. It was nice and sunny today, but the winds were straight out of the south. The snow is still soft, which makes setting up the tent easy, but biking hard.

With the strong winds and blowing snow, navigation was easy — head straight into the blowing wind.

In a lot of ways, this feels like the first couple of weeks, only colder. It feels like I am always climbing, but it is just the soft snow and wind. I gain a hundred feet and then lose it over and over. Fortunately I am now better at working with my gear and sleds and don't spend as much time adjusting things. Still, it is hard to be back to getting low mileage. Half a degree to go... not long now.

Congratulations to Juan for finishing his skiing/biking expedition. He has accomplished a great feat, because traveling to the South Pole is challenging. When I spoke with him at the beginning of our separate journeys, he told me that he would not say he did something that he didn't do. He knows, as do others, how much biking he really did, so now is the time for him to do the honorable thing and be honest in his claims.

Daniel would later say, "I was getting reports back to me that Juan was claiming to have biked to the South Pole. His expedition was difficult and an incredible feat. However, there is no way that it should be considered a bike expedition. A few weeks after I got home, I got an email from Guinness World Records asking about my expedition because they thought maybe it would qualify as a record, but that there were two others claiming to be the first. I can understand Maria's claim, but I find it incredible that Juan would make that claim."

Forum/Delorme — 18 January 2014:

Not too many people arrive at that man made little shiny orb at the bottom of the globe under their own power.

My hat is off to anyone who has tried or made it there under their own two foot power for sure, there are some ridiculously harsh conditions there on the best of days.

Journal — 19 January 2014:

S89° 39.396′ W070° 56.714 11.6nm 9106 feet 23.8 to go

It was a mix of sunny and white out today. I had fun in the first half of the day figuring out different ways to navigate. Yesterday I had been following truck tracks but they went way off course so eventually I went out on my own so there were no ski or truck tracks to follow. I had that same situation before I got to the road before patriot Hills, but there were mountains to be able to navigate with. Here, there is nothing but snow. Anyway it was fun until late in the day when I got real hungry.

The return of Truman.

The reality show feeling so well expressed by Truman was coming back right here at the end. As Daniel blogged in his tent at night, he got more and more followers who were vicariously cycling with him up the ice to the pole. He said, "I just turned my life into *The Truman Show.*"

More than 700 miles of riding left Daniel's body low on energy. His supplies were dwindling and he still had 24 miles to go.

I am out of food. Actually I have two freeze-dried meals left but nothing to eat while I bike and no punch or chocolate for my water. So I was trying to go until 9 p.m. when I would set up a tent and sleep then eat a meal. But at 6:30 I completely ran out of energy, felt sick and took a while before I could recover. I set up the tent and then went through all my garbage and ate all the crumbs etc. left behind in the packages. That is dinner tonight. In the morning I will eat one meal, hope I can get another 11.6 miles eat the last meal and see if I can finish.

With the end so close, yet so far, Burton could only think, "What if I'm the guy who makes it within 100 miles of the South Pole, but can't quite finish it?" The thought was debilitating, but the fear of failure drove him on. He kept pedaling.

Burton had already missed Thanksgiving (spent in Chile), his 50th birthday (on his second day of riding in Antarctica), his wedding anniversary, Christmas, New Year's, his wife's birthday, and his son's birthday. At least he would make it home in time for Groundhog Day, he told himself.

Daniel says, "Most people don't think of Groundhog Day as being a major holiday, but it is one of our favorite holidays. We watch the movie *Groundhog Day* each year. In the movie, Ralph orders flapjacks. One year when we got to this part, I jumped up and fixed pancakes for everyone. Ever since then we have had a big family celebration on Groundhog Day and eat breakfast food for dinner. It was cool to get home in time for the family Groundhog Day party. "

Daniel was floating along in a dream…or was it a trance? Maybe it was just a zen dedication. He knew it was real because he recorded it in his blog.

Blog—13 January 2014:

There has been a light snow fall and lots of clouds the last few days. The result is the softest snow I've had to deal with for a long time. Also, as I was sleeping and when I awoke today the wind was blowing. However, when I started riding the wind died down and it seemed there was always just enough of a break in the clouds all day to provide me with enough light to see. I am very grateful for this.

Forum/Delorme—19 January 2014:

I arrived at the Amundsen–Scott South Pole Station aboard a plane on Dec 17, 1984 (Summer) and stayed in a Jamesway construction camp for 3 weeks.

Let me tell you something, if you walk out to the 'Pole' on a 'best day' you would seriously re-think even considering arriving to this location on 'foot' from any compass point by any conveyance from the coast.

It's a blindingly vast white plain in all directions and technically the largest desert on earth.

One of the most wickedly awesome sights in my wanderings I have ever seen.

I can't even fathom trying to ride a 'fat tired' bike from Hercules Inlet to there.

Blog — 19 January 2014:

Fun! Fun! Fun!

S89° 39.396 W070° 56.714 11.6 nm Elev. 9,106 ft. 28 miles to go.

Most of the time I have been able to follow the tracks from the ski expeditions and the tracks left behind by the arctic trucks. However the track I was following yesterday was headed too far east. So I had to leave the track and am now traveling without any tracks to follow. I didn't have any tracks to follow at the beginning near Patriot Hills, but I could use the mountains to help navigate. Now there is nothing but snow. Yesterday, I used the wind to navigate, but it was a bit of a crosswind today and was not good for navigating. So I had a lot of fun trying different methods of using my compass and my GPS for navigation. It was a bit like a kid playing in the snow.

Daniel reflects, "One of the cool things about my final route into the pole is that it took me to a place where it is highly unlikely that anybody had ever been before. Kind of a cool thing."

Today was a mix of sunshine and whiteout. There is still soft snow so biking is hard and I once again got low mileage. Sometimes I wonder if I will ever get to the end. I now have only two meals remaining, so I need to finish soon.

Blog AND Journal — 20 January 2014:

Dumb Dan, Thanks Hannah[28]!!

S89° 44.070 W076° 5.711 Elev. 9,179 ft 7.5 nm 18.3 miles remaining

Journal:

Last night, I called in to ALE to tell them I am out of food. They told me to call them in the morning and give them my location and they would send Hannah down on a snowmobile with more food. I figured that if I was in truck tracks I would be able to travel faster and that maybe there would be truck tracks on my preplanned route. So in the morning I ate my last two meals and instead of heading south I went west to get back on my route. I saw a few ski expedition tracks heading south as I went west but continued on hoping for

---

[28] Hannah McKeand nordic skied in 2006 from the coast at Hercules Inlet to the South Pole by herself, 630 *nautical* miles over the wind blasted crystalline ice sheet of Antarctica, setting the record for the fastest journey by a man or woman.

truck tracks. When I got to my preplanned route there were no truck tracks, and no ski tracks. I then called in to give my coordinates so Hannah could find me. She, however, had already left and gone to my prior camping area and was following my tracks trying to find me.

Dan pointed out, "This was one day away from the South Pole. If I hadn't had to go off route to get my last cache I would have arrived at the Pole before running out of food. I also would not have learned what it was like to eat garbage, and I would not have known the joy of having Hannah give me what has to be the most beloved bottle of Coke of all time.

"I had gone through as much food as possible when I picked up the third cache to reduce weight. I had figured I would already be at the pole by now. But instead, I was running really low on food. I was working on stretching out the food as best as I could. I got to where I had 3 meals left and needed to get 12.6 miles between meals in order to finish. I ate all my garbage one night for dinner, cutting open the empty food packages, and getting the little bits of frozen food left in the corners. Then I ate one meal for breakfast. I then was only able to get about 11 miles out of the breakfast meal before I nearly passed out from lack of energy and had to stop. (BONK!)"

Too late, Daniel remembered his canyon training in Utah. From the blog:

> Mike Boyd says that the hill from Elberta to Eureka takes one hour no matter how hard you push. One time, I tried to climb the hill as fast as I could. I figured I could recover while I waited for him and Bob to climb the hill. I, of course, was wrong and I had a really hard time finishing the ride.

Back in Antarctica, the famous Hannah from ALE showed up like a Mother Teresa for South Pole pilgrims on their last legs, with a bunch of food—candy, cookies, sandwiches, and chocolate bars for Daniel.

Blog:

> She found me when I was 19.1 miles from the South Pole and she gave me about 50 pounds of food.
>
> I was so excited about all the great treats she was giving me that I set up my tent right then and I ate and ate and ate. Once I did that, I had to dry out all of my gear before I could go again, or else with how cold it

was I would freeze to death. So I tried to get a little sleep, but I couldn't fall asleep. So I packed up the tent and started my last push to the South Pole.

Another forum of extreme athletes and merchants of exotic expeditionary equipment began to light up. It was like the crowd gathering at the finish line as the contestants come into view.

Forum/Delorme — 20 January 2014:

It looks like Daniel is getting nearer the Pole slowly but surely…

Journal — 20 Jan 2014:

I've done a few dumb things. First, early in the expedition I had extra food, so at the halfway resupply, I sent a lot of food back to base camp. Then at the three-quarter resupply, I went through my food and fuel as fast as I could to reduce my weight. I thought I would be done a week ago. I had some extra food in case I didn't make it as soon as I thought. Well, this morning I ate my remaining food. Part of the problem I've had the past couple of days is I didn't have enough food to keep my pace.

As Daniel totaled up his miles for each day, he realized he could not reach the Pole before his food ran out and before the last flight of the season could extract him back to civilization. He had to calculate a new daily mileage goal and hit that target not consistently, but constantly, or he wouldn't get on that plane home.

After I ran out of food, Hannah from ALE came to my rescue with new food. I then set up my tent and went through the food. I said in my blog entry that I got some sleep while my clothes were drying. I really wanted to sleep, but it just wouldn't come to me, so I headed south. After about six miles, I reached the top of a hill and I could see the South Pole Station. I broke down in emotional joy. I then went for a short distance, and for some reason it became very difficult to move forward. It took me a while to realize what was wrong. The rear tire had gone completely flat. I quickly changed the flat.

The next dumb thing that I did was to follow some truck track until it took me over six miles off course. I then headed toward my next way point which is at the start of the corridor that you have to use to go to the pole. That was a good choice, but this morning I took a gamble and decided to return to my planned route. This meant going west three miles, but the corridor is east of where I was, so this was

a bit of going the wrong direction. I was hoping that it would be worth going the wrong direction if I could get back on the track left by the arctic trucks. But when I reached my planned route there were no tracks. I then continued on the planned route, but by then I was tired and out of strength.

Now, Daniel stood on the pedals of his bike and drove his legs up the penultimate hill, thirteen miles from the Pole. The only sound in this environment was the crunch of his knobby, treaded tires through the crystalline snow and the huff puff of his breath, which froze and fell to the snow right out of his mouth. He put his belly core and his rocking shoulders into it in order to drag his little convoy up…and up.

Blog:

I have to call in to the base camp and let them know I am okay at 9:40 p.m. (Chilean time) each day. Failing to call in can trigger a search and rescue operation, and of course I don't want to do that. So after the call in, I will pack up my tent and get going again. With fewer than 20 miles to go, Hannah's tracks to follow, and candy and trail mix to keep my energy up, I should be able to finish biking through the night and into tomorrow. My plan is to keep going until I get to the South Pole, so my next blog entry should be at the South Pole.

Hannah's tracks made it so I didn't have to navigate, but the track left by the snowmobile was terrible to bike on, so the best conditions were just outside of the track the snowmobile left behind.

Daniel Burton was coming in from the profound and total aloneness of the ultimate quiet. Daniel relates, "A glacier is a frozen river. Antarctica is a frozen sea. The sastrugi are frozen waves. Rolling over the 'swells,' one inhabits the circle of the horizon. The edge of the world is right there in all directions. I think I'm climbing, yet the GPS says I'm descending. I look back. It is too hard to tell what is up and what is down. I went over the Transantarctic Mountains and never saw them because they are buried under the ice."

Vesa Luomala of Helsinki, Finland had this to say about Antarctica, "I think there is no room for underestimating a place like Antarctica. I have faced a Piteraq and [a] few other strong storms in Greenland and know what it might be at worst… Still, I think the biggest challenge for me will be the solitude. On the other hand, that is what I want to explore here."

Daniel's Blog:

Feeling good about my odds of finishing the first *real* bicycle riding expedition to the South Pole tomorrow. However, keep following these posts, as I will be adding some pictures and have a few things to announce, like a return party.

Here was an interplanetary alien exploring an empty white world. Here was one lone human, isolated from all his kind, without his pack, without his band, connected with his fellow beings across the atmosphere electromagnetically and spiritually. It was a moment to savor, to listen to the silence and see the white surface under the blue sky. But he had better not stop to listen and gaze for more than the time it takes to catch his breath.

Keep going to the top. At the top you will see where you are and orient yourself to an actual place instead of pedaling through a pearly limbo.

Daniel got up on the crest and kept going until he was sure his sleds were on the level with him. Only then did he stop. Daring greatly (what a tragedy it would be to freeze to death now), he put his right foot down on the snow and sat motionless on his bike. There was the South Pole

Station! Just thirteen miles away! Overwhelmed with joy, Daniel pulled out his Iridium satellite phone and called his wife. In their house in Eagle Mountain, Utah, the wife of the Antarctic explorer-adventurer jumped for the home phone when her husband called on the sat phone. "It was about 11:00 at night and Media was lying in bed," Daniel reported. "She says I was excited and she could hear me say, 'I can see it; I can see the South Pole!' She could tell I was in tears and could hardly get the words out. And then the line went dead. Like most other times I called, the phone call ended with the connection being dropped.

After 50 days of riding and with only 13 more miles to go, the buildings at the South Pole began breaking up the white, barren landscape.

Daniel peered south and all he could see were three small dots on the horizon. Daniel remembers, "At first I thought maybe it was sastrugi, but after a few minutes I could tell that it was actually the South Pole Station." Daniel was seeing the station telescope observatory and a large antenna of the 2009 main building up on giant stilts to keep the whole habitable structure out of the deepest winter snow. Daniel rolled down his last hill and pedaled and pushed the final thirteen miles toward the three dots, which grew in size and detail with every revolution of his big wheeled fat tires.

Pedal on! No more up, only down! But then Daniel was appalled to see…he wasn't on the last hill. He had to slide down a big dip and then climb once more up to the level plain of South Pole Station. After a while he started going south again, but he couldn't look out to the right where the South Pole was without being overwhelmed with joy.

Forum/Delorme—21 January 2014 - 5:21 pm:

He must be there by now. I looked a few minutes ago and his inreach most recent track point was 89.999946 south. But his last blog entry was from last night.

"After fixing a flat I continued on to the pole. When I rolled to a stop, nobody was there. The camp of ALE had been packed up and flown out the day before. As the South Pole Station was on New Zealand time, it was the middle of their night. I went and checked out the South Pole marker. I had actually arrived at the South Pole! But then, instead of being excited I was feeling like, OK I made it. Now what?"

Daniel sent a message to his wife telling her he had arrived. "The night before, she had told the kids that I could see the South Pole.

"The next day as she was at school [she is a math teacher] she spent the morning popping her head into the various classrooms and telling the other teachers that I was close and that I would probably get there that day. When she received the call that I had finally arrived, she was still at school. Media was excited and went through the teachers' lounge and through the halls telling everyone, 'He made it to the South Pole! He is there!'"

How many movies have there been where the space explorers come to the earth outpost on another planet and find that their people are nowhere to be found? Antarctica is almost another planet. It is another world. Daniel the 'bike-o-naut' made it to the outpost of civilization, which was…seemingly abandoned. Did he arrive in time to catch the plane or was he marooned?

"What an anti-climax… joy and celebrations among my family and friends nearly nine thousand miles away from the South Pole when I first saw the station, but 'Who are you again?' when I stood looking up at its sleek, ultra contemporary, metal and composition techno-building gleaming silver and polished gray in the unimpeded sunshine."

Off to the right side from Daniel's point of view was the "antenna farm" of communication domes and satellite dishes for 21st century communications and atmospheric, experimental data collection. In the other direction, there was a big, empty, "vacant lot." There were signs saying that this was a no go area because of the danger of falling through the ice into the remaining holes in the ice where the South Pole Station of the 1970s had been. That main building had been a geodesic dome used as an astronomic and weather observatory. The geodesic dome building had been completely dismantled. There was nothing where it had been.

So this was the "Amundsen-Scott South Pole Station," first planted at the South Pole by the U.S. Navy in 1956 and named for Roald Amundsen and Robert Scott who were the first to race to the Pole. Now Daniel Burton was the latest, although certainly not the last.

Roald Amundsen led four men on his Norwegian expedition to reach the Geographic South Pole in December, 1911. Robert F. Scott, whose British "Terra Nova" expedition of Scott and five men reached the South Pole about one month later (in January 1912), just barely lost the race to become the first people? ever to reach the South Pole. Scott's expedition also lost their lives during the journey back to the coast, while all of Amundsen's expedition returned safely to their base. The first expeditions came to the bays and inlets of the Antarctic coast in sailing ships and trekked to the Pole on long, wooden, Nordic skis and with ponies and dog sleds. Daniel's fellow expeditionaries did it with combinations of skis, bicycles and even tricycles. Daniel, of course, was there to prove and, in fact, had proved that it could be done solely with the proper kind of snow bike.

Amundsen and Scott were as cut off from human society as if they had crashed on another planet. Daniel and the others were as connected as if they rode on the Mars rover, with satellite phones and GPS navigation, not to mention iPads, iPhones, and iTunes. But even Amundsen, Scott, and Daniel's competitors had not done it all by means of one person on one bicycle, wheels rolling the entire distance. Daniel Burton was not a cross country skier; he was not a snowshoer; he was not a recumbent trike expert; he was a cyclist. He rode bikes down roads and up mountains. Now he had ridden his bicycle some of every day all alone from the perimeter of the Antarctic continent to the South Pole, the first and only person to accomplish that feat.

Blog — 21 January 2014:

I'M AT THE SOUTH POLE!!!!!!!

S90° 00.000

The South Pole station came into view when I was about 13 nautical miles away. When I saw it, I was so overcome with joy! I called home to my wife and lost all control of my emotions. The black dots on the horizon were the most wonderful thing I have ever seen. It was starting to feel like I would never make it.

I am now at the pole and have set up camp. I need to find where they cached my clean clothes and other items. I made a quick visit to the actual pole marker, but will go back later and bike around the pole to the song *Around the World* after I get all my batteries charged. I am so happy to have finally finished biking to the pole, going the full distance, 100% by bicycle.

Enough of this for now. Daniel had to look for where he was supposed to check in off the ice and get temporary visitor's quarters. He came rolling in out of the wilderness into what he had been told would be a summer camp of temporary tents. Here, visitors in from their expeditions could stay until the last plane out. Daniel entered the site he had been so looking forward to living in only to see that the tent city was gone. There was only the packed snow where the structures had been just a day before. ALE had "struck the tents" as pioneers and other trekkers would say. Daniel realized, "My visitor quarters would be my own tent that I had taken with me from the coast. There were a lot of science experiments going on, so there were poles marking the very specific area where I was allowed to camp." This was not exactly a ticker tape parade for the first person to trek from the Antarctic coast to the South Pole completely by bicycle.

Blog—21 January 2014:

It is COLD here!

Hannah gave me a bottle of Coke with the food she brought yesterday. I warmed it up before I started this morning and then packed it in the middle of my parka. It was still warm when I got it out, but before I could unscrew the lid it turned to slush. Almost like the liquid nitrogen tricks. It is COLD here.

I'm sure I'll miss people, but I'll try to recognize everyone as soon as I can. For now—

Thanks to my family for their love, patience and support!

Super big thank you to all the guys who've run my bike store while I've been gone: Jake, Greg, John, Joel, Steve, Ron, and Myron.

Thank you to everyone who donated to my expedition at GoFundMe!

A special shout out to all of my sponsors! Please support them if you can—and let your friends and neighbors know about them, too.

Dreamy blogging:

Am I a Pro Athlete?

The following scene was repeated throughout my childhood. Sometimes it was for football, or baseball, or basketball, volleyball, steal the flag or even just tag, but whatever the team event the general plot was the same.

First, the two self-declared best athletes would be designated as team captains. Then everyone else would stand in a big group and wait as the captains would alternate choosing who would be on their team. It wouldn't take long before those that were clearly the best were chosen and then the average people would start to get picked. I always thought that was where I belonged, somewhere in the middle of the pack.

After a while though, the average athletes were all gone and the captains would start picking through the mediocre people. Well, I think I am better than that, but I can live with being picked out of that group. Soon all those are gone and now all that remains are those that they take onto their team because they have to. It is sad that I am amongst those, but, hey, if I get to play that is OK. Then it gets down to the real dregs of the group, a couple of real losers, and I think to myself, "How could you have picked him over me?" Finally it is down to the last two people—you've got to be kidding me! The worst kid in the whole group gets picked before me.

The game starts. If it is football, nobody pays any attention to me. They hike the ball and I easily slip through the offensive line and tackle the quarterback. I guess they figure it is a fluke and still ignore me. After sacking the quarterback a few times, they put someone on me and put an end to my sacking. Surely, though, I am helping the team by tying up a player that could be doing something else. Next time I will get picked earlier. But it never turns out that way.

Same basic thing happens in other games. If it is steal the flag, everyone has forgotten what team got stuck with me and I easily walk back to the flag, grab it and run. I make good progress at getting the flag across the line, but yet again nobody seems to appreciate my contribution to the team.

Maybe I *am* the worst athlete. After all, I was the last kid in the neighborhood to learn to ride a bike. Eight years old, and kids half my age are riding around on bikes, and I have a great big trike.

When I start mountain biking with the guys at Novell, they seem impressed with how quickly I go from a beginner to riding with almost keeping up with the most serious riders. Before long, I get this strange reputation as being an advanced mountain biker. I invite someone to go biking with us and get turned down because they feel they can't ride at my level. I know that it really isn't because I am that good, but rather it is because I am hanging out with others that are that good.

So here I am, somewhere out on the Polar Plateau, biking towards the South Pole. Is it possible that I am a professional athlete? When my

Shimano rep handed over the donations from Shimano, he told me that they only do this for professional athletes. "Wow!" I thought, "It is cool that they are making this exception." He continues to tell me of the feedback that Shimano and Pearl Izumi want on how their products work for me.

As I worked on getting all the gear for the expedition, I requested a sponsorship from a lot of companies and got turned down by most. Columbia said I could make a submission for their pro program. When I filled out the forms, it asked what category I was applying as. The best fit I could find was a pro athlete. When they accepted my application to be considered a pro athlete I was a bit impressed.

That was when I was simply talking about what I was planning on doing. Now that I am here, is it really possible that the last guy chosen for any team—the computer geek—is it possible that he is a professional athlete?

Thank you to those sponsors and companies that had faith in me. And thank you to all of you family, friends and supporters who have cheered me on throughout this journey.

Blog—23 January 2014:

Back at Union Glacier Camp

Okay, I'm finally getting sleepy. I have completely lost track of time and days. It could be said that it is still the same day that it was when I arrived here back in November, as the sun has not set once since I've been here. But to me, though, the last few days, I can't tell how many they were and what was what day.

When I arrived at the South Pole I sat around in my tent eating and maybe getting a bit of a nap. Then my new best friend, Vesa Luomala [solo ski, from Finland] arrived. A little after that, we visited the South Pole Station. We took pictures of each other at the pole, and I gathered up as many snowmen as I could. I packed up my tent and we flew back to the Union Glacier base camp.

Correne Coetzer of ExplorersWeb wrote:

On December 1st, Vesa started off from Hercules Inlet and completed the 1130 km on January 22nd at 15h02 Chilean time, he reports. He completed the route solo, unassisted and unsupported. He and Daniel Burton had a tour of the South Pole Station and were to be picked up soon after that by the ALE plane as the weather was deteriorating, which would delay a return to Union Glacier.

The day before Vesa arrived at the SP he saw the Station, 'It looked so different (from what) I had imagined...like I had walked into Star Wars movie. There were a lot of futuristic buildings in hill opposite to me.

Back at the Union Glacier base camp Daniel also blogged.

Everything is in cleanup mode here. I took so long that Vesa and I are the last two non-ALE people left. I have been hanging around doing anything besides setting up my tent yet again. To get this blog entry sent, and to try to send a few pictures, I have to leave this dining tent, since the insulation is also a radio shield. It has been a long journey.

The next flight out of Antarctica is on January 27, so I am here for a few more days.

Sorry, but I can't seem to get any pictures sent. The batteries don't like having been frozen, and they simply aren't charging. I will keep trying to get something sent.

Pensive meditation blog — 24 January 2014:

Ghost Camp

It's almost like a little Ghost Town here now. I'm waiting for my flight back to Chile which is scheduled for the 27th, but may get bumped to the 26th because of weather. In the meantime, they are in the process of taking down camp and getting everything ready to be sent back to Chile until next season. So it is continually getting to be less and less of a camp.

It's not too bad outside here right now, just a little below freezing. Much warmer than it was at the pole. Vesa told me today that the temperature inside his tent was 80 degrees. I had to open the flaps on my tent because it was so warm inside.

I've been trying and trying to send pictures, but I just can't get a good enough charge on my batteries to be able to send them. Minus 40 degrees is very hard on batteries. After I get to Chile I can send some pictures. I don't know when I will fly home to Utah yet. I am waiting to buy a return flight ticket until I know for sure when I will be back in Chile. The flights out of Antarctica can be delayed because of weather and that has happened a lot this year.

What can I do with this? What good is it? What good am I?

When Daniel finally got back to Chile he blogged,

The End of a Very Long Day

I feel like Phil in the movie *Goundhog Day*. This is the end of a very long day. It started almost two months ago and finally it is dark. The first night I have had since last November. Yet I have been spending so much time posting replies to comments and posting pictures to Facebook and stuff like that that I am still awake at 3:34 am. I need to get to bed. Soon. Mike says I look like a homeless dude and he wants to give me $5. I'll take it.

But, whether my wife likes it or not, the beard stays until I go to church at least once. It is a bit of an expedition trophy. I have my tent and everything spread all over my room here in Punta Arenas to dry out. When they brought my bike to my room I went down to the bike shop where a cassette and cassette lock ring tool were purchased to thank them and to get a bolt I lost on the trip. I tried to tell them thanks and let them know they are part of history by making the first bike expedition to the South Pole a success but I don't think they understood what I was saying. I love Punta Arenas, but it is sometimes hard when my Spanish is near zero and people don't speak English here.

I'm tired and going to get some sleep, I'll start adding pictures into the blog posts tomorrow. In the mean time I posted some higher res pictures on Facebook.

Blog — 27 January 2014:

The Body Strikes Back

I think my body is still in rebellion. My pants fit like I'm Harry Potter and my pants are Dudley hand-me-downs. My few hour bike ride today has made my legs very weak and tired, and this morning I about passed out on the way to breakfast. A little orange juice fixed this morning's problem.

One day, before I left Chile for Antarctica, I had ice cream for lunch and ice cream soup for dinner. I went and had pizza with Vesa just a little bit ago, and was very full. But now I am already hungry again, so I am doing the ice cream/ice cream soup thing again tonight. I also got a few other high sugar items to keep me going until morning. It is just too long between meals right now to go all night without eating.

Blog—29 January 2014:

Cold tiles

Cold floor tiles in the morning are no problem when your feet are mostly numb.

I stayed up all night talking to my daughter's boyfriend. I really should get more rest. Today I need to get all my stuff into a box and shipped back home, and then catch a flight home myself. Oh yeah, and see if I can get someone to ask the "Firgadorific" company, in Spanish, if they can help me find my GPS. I'm pretty sure the security guards picked it up but I don't know enough Spanish to ask if they found it and to offer them a reward for its return.

Blog—2 February 2014

I'm home! Sorry for the lack of posts. Just nice to recover a bit. I did add a post today about the welcome home party.

Daniel loved the professional questions from people who shared his experience, but he struggled to talk sense to them. He realized it was alienation.

Daniel blogged out a simple thought to the nation of followers.

Forum/Delorme—24 January 2014:

TEAM SERIOUS Final Report

That's some good old fashioned great adventure going on right there.

Congratulations to Mr. Burton for being the 1st person to make it from the Antarctic coast to the South Pole under his own power via bicycle only.

Welcome to the shiny orb at the bottom of the globe my friend.

The fuzziness of the journey will fade, but that place never will.

Daniel replied back—16 June 2014:

I just found this forum thread. Thanks for following. Thoughts about above posts:

GPS works great at the South Pole. I had two Garmin GPSs for navigating, one of my cameras had a gps in it, and the two satellite phones also had GPS in them. They all worked just fine at the South Pole. The mapping "failed" in that it was the wrong kind of map to use at the South Pole, but there is no way to get the DeLorme site to use an azimuthal projection.

It was a great adventure and hopefully it inspires others to go out and do great things."

Team Serious came back with:

Navigation and communication aside, bloody good show ol' chap

Congratulations Dan. That was one…bike ride

As said, even contemplating a bike ride from Hercules Inlet to the "shiny orb" has my hat tipped towards you.

Daniel Burton became the first explorer to truly ride a bicycle to the South Pole. He blogged with humility but with self respect,

Two other cycling expeditions to the South Pole started this year. One woman [Maria Leijerstam] rode a special tricycle on a packed road with constant support from an accompanying truck. She travelled a little more than 300 miles—less than half the distance I rode from Hercules Inlet. A man from Spain [Juan Menéndez Granados] traveled the same route as I did, but used skis to aid his excursion. Most of his trip was done on skis—pulling his sled with his bike in the sled, rather than riding it [a much easier method]. The man from Spain also skied exclusively during the first 10 days, never riding his bike during the hardest part of the journey.

Many people have skied to the South Pole, but Daniel Burton of Eagle Mountain became the first person to ride a bicycle from Hercules Inlet to the South Pole—more than 750 miles. He did it by relying on strong legs, endurance, faith, and his refusal to accept failure as an option.

Daniel concluded his motivational planning by blogging,

There are three great adventurers that were the inspiration for my expedition,

Eric Larsen

In December 2012, just as I was getting into snow biking, Eric started his expedition to bike to the South Pole. I followed his expedition. In 8 days he traveled one fourth of the way to the South Pole. It took me sixteen days to cover the same distance. I would never have even thought about biking to the South Pole if I hadn't heard of Eric's expedition. I studied his blog to learn as much as I could about biking to the South Pole. While I was on my expedition I would often remember things I had read in his blog, and think that now I understood what he was talking about. Eric is a true inspiration and his expedition convinced me that biking to the South Pole was possible.

Hannah McKeand

Hannah used to hold the record for the fastest solo expedition to the South Pole. I read her blog and learned a lot about polar expeditions from it. I was very honored to have her bring me food when I ran out one day before I reached the pole.

Aaron Linsdau

He was the man who would not quit... would not let his brain think the thought. He had the pattern of mental training more important than any physical training I could do. I would motivate myself to push through to the finish in the manner of Aaron.

There are many great explorers but those three are the ones that inspired me the most as I biked to the South Pole. Thanks Eric, Hannah, and Aaron!

What is the Lesson? What is the Value?

With this achievement, Daniel Burton learned many things of value to us all. He learned that a fifty-year-old man could do this with age being immaterial to the level of fitness required. He learned that, with the proper physical, mental, emotional, and spiritual preparation and a way of working that ensured the solution to any problem that rose up before him, he could and did do the impossible.

Daniel Burton said of his bicycle ride from the coast of Antarctica to the South Pole, "I did it, but really I am just like everybody else." Looking back on his expedition to the South Pole, Daniel said, "If I had acknowledged at the beginning that I could fail, then I would have failed." The thought process of self-conviction started when he formed the intention to cycle to the South Pole.

Energy Solutions was the only company that would give him a monetary sponsorship because nobody believed he could do it. So he borrowed eighty thousand dollars and he did it. That is the essential truth. All the details are for accuracy and credibility, but this is the essence, *he did it.*

If the thousands of people who followed Daniel's course into history get nothing else from his story, they will ponder his web admonition to them: "Remember to get out and be active."

A few months after Daniel returned from the South Pole, he came across a Mtbr Forum talking about the thee cycling expeditions, and added his own comment to the end of the forum thread,

"I just read this thread for the first time. Very entertaining. It is fun to see all the things people said about me and also about Juan and Maria.

"As far as I know, Maria pedaled the whole distance to the South Pole, the only one of us to do that. From what her driver said, the trike worked great on her route but would not have been capable of doing the Hercules route. The compacted road was critical to her success. I also understand that she did get into the truck to rest (great way to keep from freezing to death, and by death I mean death) but that the truck never moved her forward.

"The route Juan and I took was more of an expedition than a bike ride. It required that we navigate, avoid crevasses, deal with sastrugi, and travel an uncompacted wilderness route. There is no way you can really understand what this was like unless you have done an expedition to the South Pole yourself.

"There have been many people that have gone solo with no resupplies to the South Pole. There is even a person (Helen Skelton, in 2012) that skied and biked to the South Pole. The point of my expedition was to bike to the South Pole, which I did. I had three (well really four) resupplies, and I pushed my bike (hike-a-bike) A LOT. However, my wheels rolled the whole distance and I rode my bike every day. I did not compromise my stated expedition in order to make it first. I pushed when I had to and rode (pedaled) whenever possible. Some days that meant I would pedal for about 10 feet before getting stuck in soft snow, recover, and then pedal again for another 10 feet. Other days I would be able to ride for miles without stopping.

"In spite of what has been said, I was well prepared for the expedition. I did not take two of everything with me. That would be stupid. I was prepared to fix a frozen hub, but I did not anticipate that I would break the hub body into a bunch of little pieces. However I was prepared to finish with what I had. Fortunately they were able to get a new wheel to me, which made this much nicer. Dropping off of six foot sastrugi was a lot nicer when I was able to stop pedaling and get behind my seat. (Dropping off sastrugi with a functioning wheel was one of the few parts of the expedition that was actually fun.)

"Why two sleds? I had the ability to put all my stuff into one sled. I also could put most of my stuff in my panniers and make my sleds very light. The thing is NOBODY knew what would work best in Antarctica. Eric was convinced that panniers was the best route, and up until my expedition he had more experience with biking to the South Pole than anyone else. In fact, I think he still has the second longest cycling expedition in Antarctica after mine. I think he traveled farther by bike in his attempt than Maria travelled. I took his advice and had panniers. I also took two sleds so I could work out what was best. It turned out two sled was much better than one sled. Balancing the weight between the two sleds, and getting rid of the panniers was the best method.

"I had a lot of advice from people that had a lot of polar experience. I ignored advice from people I did not know, and took the advice of people that were experts in Antarctican expeditions that worked with me to make this expedition possible. The people that work for ALE were great!

"I was by far the least experienced expedition to the South Pole this past season (ski, bike, or truck). I had no prior polar experience; I hadn't done any other real expeditions; I was definitely the rookie. I am simply an average person who was given a chance to do something super cool. However, I know how to survive in the wilderness, and I am really good at solving problems. I planned and prepared well for the expedition, and in the end the preparations I made were what I needed. In reality, the most important training I did was mental. There are a lot of amazing explorers in this world. I met a bunch of them in Antarctica. When I sat down with those amazing mountaineer and polar adventurers, I felt like a midget amongst giants."

Daniel Burton did make it to the South Pole on his bicycle in time to board the rugged little wilderness beating De Havilland Canada DHC-3 Otter sent by the Antarctic Logistics and Expeditions Corporation. Also jumping on board was the great Finnish Nordic skier, Vesa Luomala, who had just been the first Finn to ski from the coast to the South Pole, solo, unassisted, no resupplies. Daniel observed that Vesa had skied from coast to pole almost as fast as Daniel had cycled from coast to pole, but the *principle of doing an extraordinary feat first was the same in both cases.*

Here is a lesson. Quit when you're ahead. "Eventually we flew back to Chile. I had been all the way to the South Pole and had not seen any penguins so I decided to go find a penguin colony. I thought, 'If I can bike to the South Pole, surely I can bike 30 miles to a penguin colony.'

"Along the way, I talked to a couple of young men and figured out I was still headed the right direction. A little while after I left them, I looked down and my GPS was gone. It must have fallen out when I laid the bike down to talk to them. So I went back,t hey were gone and some older gentleman was there. I couldn't figure out how to get him to realize that I had dropped the GPS and the other two must have picked it up. So I lost the GPS with all my South Pole trip data on it! I want that back so much! If I could figure out how to offer the security guards a reward for the return of the GPS I would.

"I eventually gave up and in a bit of a sad mood continued on. It was windy. It was always windy there. The tailwind turned into a crosswind with a bit of headwind. I remembered why I got rid of the panniers at Thiel. They were so hard to move into a headwind. I was biking with a 30° lean to the left and kept getting blown off the street. I realized I was not enjoying this. I had biked for two months with bad winds and no penguin was going to be cute enough to make this worthwhile. So, about half way to the penguin colony I turned back, leaned 30° to the right and pedaled along. When I got to the airport I grabbed a taxi and went back to the hotel.

No penguin pictures, no fun, and now no GPS data." CRAP! as the Mormons say.

Helpful Anonymous 1—January 30, 2014 at 3:01 PM

Ask them about the GPS and offer a reward, say this (spelled phonetically): "Say pear-dee-OH la hey-pay-essay day me bee-see-CLAY-tah. Eye oon pro-PEE-no poor en-cone-TRAR-low. (Se perdio la GPS de mi bicicleta. Hay un propino por encontrarlo.) Good luck."

Helpful Anonymous 2—January 31, 2014 at 9:50 AM

Print this question out and show it to them:

"Hace unos días perdí mi GPS, ¿conoces a alguien que se encuentra uno?"

Daniel wrote in his blog:

I'm sure everyone is familiar with Aesop's fable of the Fox and the Grapes. But if not, here it is:

ONE hot summer's day a Fox was strolling through an orchard till he came to a bunch of Grapes just ripening on a vine which had been trained over a lofty branch. "Just the things to quench my thirst," quoth he. Drawing back a few paces, he took a run and a jump, and just missed the bunch. Turning round again with a One, Two, Three, he jumped up, but with no greater success. Again and again he tried after the tempting morsel, but at last had to give it up, and walked away with his nose in the air, saying: "I am sure they are sour."

Moral : "It is easy to despise what you cannot get."

I had a lot of people tell me that I was crazy for wanting to bike to the South Pole. A neighbor simply told me, "DON'T GO!" I had others that asked if I would leave the bike store to them in the case that I died. I thought it was a joke, but maybe it was a more serious request than I thought, because I was told when I returned that they really did think I would die.

I received a lot of criticism. Fortunately for me one of my biggest detractors posted to a public forum, thus preserving his words. He said:

"Until recently I had been plotting, planning and working toward my own south pole attempt. Different route, different mentality, entirely different style than yours.

"I started researching every aspect from every angle back in 2004, and spent the next 6 years fiddling with gear, nutrition, and all of the little things that would ultimately give me a fighting chance once on the ice. Recently, after much thought and introspection, I've concluded that I wouldn't get enough enjoyment out of it to make it worth doing. A lack of interesting things to look at along the way is my main reason for losing interest. And that's not even factoring in the enormous cost of getting to and from the continent."

Now if that is not one of the greatest retellings of the Fox and the Grapes I don't know what is.

Biking to the South Pole was difficult beyond the wildest imagination. Every day was more difficult than I could possibly explain.

I spent 51 days alone. I fell into a crevasse. I battled headwinds that, even with my full strength, I could not push forward into. I spent many days in total whiteout, unable to see the ground I was biking over, falling off of four foot sastrugi, and worrying about what would happen if I broke a bone or broke my bike frame.

Speaking of broken bikes, I destroyed the internals of my rear hub from pedaling for up to 13 hours a day while hauling a heavy load up frozen slopes against strong headwinds. The winds were so bad that even the worst winds I have faced since I got home don't compare to the winds of Antarctica. Back to the broken hub—I ground the internals of the hub into tiny globs of black gunk. I wired my spokes to the gears so that I could continue to ride the bike. This worked... kind of. The amount of work it took to pedal was so great that it would break the wires I used to tie the gears to the spokes. I had to redo the wire job every few days. I ended up breaking three spokes before I was able to get a replacement wheel.

There is no doubt that it was an extremely difficult expedition. However, the grapes were not sour.

Antartica is beautiful beyond description. The nunataks, peaks of mountains rising above the ice cap, are majestic. The parhelia, or sun dogs, were some of the most beautiful things I have ever seen. These sun dogs were made by a full circle rainbow around the sun, with the bottom of the rainbow just touching the polar icecap. Then there was a second rainbow a little further out that arched from one point on the horizon up and above the sun and returned to the horizon. Radiating from the middle of the sun was a halo that encircled the sky. Where this halo and the rainbows intersected is where the sun dogs would hang out.

Antartica was a frozen wasteland. But there was no lack of "interesting things to look at along the way." There seemed to be an endless supply of ice drifting from the south to the north. The ice flowing in the wind formed a translucent blanket about 2 to 3 feet deep. This constant blowing ice piled up into drifts. Then on a less windy day (there were a couple of those) the sun hardened the drifting ice. Of course, the winds would return and where the drifts did not receive as much sun, and so were softer, the wind would gouge out the ice leaving behind spectacular sastrugi. While these were dangerous to bike over, especially when you could not see due to a white out, they were nonetheless spectacular. Most of the sastrugi were only a couple of feet high, but there were many that created 4 to 6 foot drops, and the largest were easily 12 feet high or more. The wind would carve some amazing shapes in the sastrugi, but the most curious one I saw looked like a penguin.

The solitude of Antartica was wonderful. I was worried before I left that being alone for that long would be difficult, but I found it to be wonderfully peaceful. The only noise was made by me. Even the wind would not make any noise unless it was from hitting me or my gear. The peace and quiet gave me abundant time to ponder.

I am not a great world traveler, but I have been to Mexico, Chile, Canada, France, Germany, and the Caribbean. While each are wonderful in their own way, there is also something common about everywhere I have been. Everywhere, that is, except Antarctica. Antarctica is like nowhere else on earth.

The grapes were truly the sweetest I have ever tasted. When I first saw the South Pole Station I was completely overwhelmed by joy. The joy of finally getting to the South Pole was more than worth the effort that it took to get there.

I just love to ride my bike

Daniel Burton, from Eagle Mountain, Utah, lived a South Pole Epic

With what do we compare this achievement? As a triumph of preparation over eventualities, it feels like Charles Lindbergh, but as an indomitable will to explore the unknown limits of the earthscape and the depth and breadth of the soulscape, it is a retelling of many stories from Caleb to Columbus, from Daniel Boone to Ernest Shackleton. In his very own odyssey, Daniel Burton, from Eagle Mountain, Utah, lived a South Pole Epic, biking for 51 days across a frozen wilderness and, as he approached the deserted camping area, all that greeted him there was a big yellow sign…

The sign read, "The world's southernmost resort."

Appendix

Antarctica Historical Firsts

17 January 1773 - James Cook and his crew crossed the Antarctic Circle

7 February 1821 - John Davis sets foot in Antarctica

1898 - Adrian de Gerlache and his men spend winter in Antarctica

1903 - Robert Falcon Scott discovers the Polar Plateau.

1909 - Earnest Shackleton is first to reach Polar Plateau reaching a point 97 nautical miles from the South Pole

16 January 1909 - Edgeworth David and team arrive at the Magnetic South Pole

14 December 1911 - Roald Amundsen and team reach the South Pole

7 January 1993 - Erling Kagge, first unassisted (no dogs, ponies, motor vehicles, etc.) to the Pole

22 January 2012 - Helen Skelton, first person to ski, bike, and kite to the Pole

26 December 2013 - Maria Leijerstam, first cycle to the South Pole

21 January 2014 - Daniel Burton, first to bike to the South Pole

Cycling Expeditions

Name	Mode	By Bike	Total	Support	Notes
Helen Skelton	Kite, Ski, Bicycle	103 miles	501 miles	Motorized Support	non coastal start
Juan Menéndez	Ski, Bicycle	<120 miles	750 miles	Solo	Hercules Inlet to Pole
Doug Stoup	Bicycle	200 miles	200 miles	Solo	Heritage Range
Eric Larsen	Bicycle	335 miles	335 miles	Solo, food drops	Hercules Inlet start
Maria Leijenstam	Tricycle	396 miles	396 miles	Motorized Support	Compacted road
Daniel Burton	Bicycle	775 miles	775 miles	Solo, food drops	Hercules Inlet to Pole

18987488R00123

Made in the USA
San Bernardino, CA
08 February 2015